In the Arresting Eye

In the
Arresting
Eye
THE RHETORIC OF IMAGISM

John T. Gage

Louisiana State University Press
Baton Rouge and London

Designer: Patricia Douglas Crowder
Typeface: VIP Bembo
Typesetter: G&S Typesetters, Inc.
Printer and Binder: Thomson-Shore, Inc.

LIBRARY OF CONGRESS CATALOGING IN PUBLICATION DATA

Gage, John, 1947–
    In the arresting eye.

    Bibliography: p.
    Includes index.
    1. Imagist poetry—History and criticism. 2. English poetry—20th century—History
and criticism. 3. American poetry—20th century—History and criticism. I. Title.
PR605.I6G3   811'.52'09   80-24893
ISBN 0-8071-0790-5

Grateful acknowledgment is made to the following for permission to quote from copyrighted
material:
    To the editors of *Style* for portions of Chapter Three which first appeared, in somewhat
different form, as "Images and Critical Method." To the editors of *Philosophy and Rhetoric* and
Pennsylvania State University Press for portions of Chapter Five which first appeared, in
somewhat different form, as "Paradoxes of Objectivity and Argument in Imagist Theory."
    RICHARD ALDINGTON: "Amalfi," "Epigrams," "Images," "Inarticulate Grief," "In the Old
Garden" ("Au Vieux Jardin"), and "London (May, 1915)," from *Images*, copyright © by Madame
Catherine Guillaume. Reprinted by permission. "Insouciance," and "Living Sepulchres" from
Images of War, copyright © by George Allen & Unwin, Publishers, Ltd. Reprinted by per-
mission.
    H. D.: "Oread," "Sea Rose," "Adonis," "Storm," "Sitalkas," "Song," "The Pool," and "Her-
monax," from *Collected Poems of H. D.*, copyright © 1925, 1953 by Norman Holmes Pearson.
"Love That I Bear," from *Selected Poems of H. D.*, copyright © 1957 by Norman Holmes Pear-
son. "If You Will Let Me Sing," from *Red Roses for Bronze*, copyright © 1931 by Norman Holmes
Pearson. Reprinted by permission of New Directions Publishing Corporation.
    T. E. HULME: "Above the Dock," "The Embankment," and prose selections from *Specula-
tions*. Reprinted by permission of Harcourt Brace Jovanovich, Inc.
    D. H. LAWRENCE: "Brooding Grief" and "Nothing to Save" from *The Complete Poems of
D. H. Lawrence*, copyright © 1964, 1971 by Angelo Ravagli and C. M. Weekly, Executors of the
Estate of Frieda Lawrence Ravagli. Reprinted by permission of Viking Penguin, Inc.
    AMY LOWELL: "The Pond," "Fugitive," "Circumstance," "Streets," "The Fisherman's Wife,"
"A Year Passes," and "Venus Transiens," from *The Complete Poetical Works of Amy Lowell*, copy-
right © 1955 by Houghton Mifflin Company. Reprinted by permission of the publisher.
    EZRA POUND: "Alba," "L'Art: 1910," "The Coming of War: Actaeon," "Fan-Piece, For her
Imperial Lord," "Gentildonna," "A Girl," "In a Station of the Metro," "Liu Ch'e," "Ts'ai Chi'h,"
and "The Return," from *Personae*, copyright © 1926 by Ezra Pound. Prose selections from
Gaudier-Brzeska: A Memoir, copyright © 1970 by Ezra Pound. Prose selections from *The Literary
Essays of Ezra Pound*, copyright © 1918, 1920, 1935 by Ezra Pound. Reprinted by permission of
New Directions Publishing Corporation, New York, and Faber and Faber, Ltd., London. All
rights reserved.
    WILLIAM CARLOS WILLIAMS: "Fire Spirit" from *The Collected Earlier Poems of William Carlos
Williams*, copyright © 1938 by New Directions Publishing Corporation. Reprinted by permis-
sion of New Directions.

for Robin and Molly

Not all our ideas, however, are thus incorporated in the fluid mass of our conscious states. Many float on the surface, like dead leaves on the water of a pond.

Henri Bergson, *Time and Free Will*

CONTENTS

PREFACE AND
ACKNOWLEDGMENTS

For reasons that I hope will become clear rather quickly, this is a polemical study. Yet I wish the reader to be aware of the nature of the polemic from the beginning. In analyzing what I consider to be the inadequacies of imagist theory, I do not wish to conclude that imagist poetry necessarily fails because of those inadequacies and should therefore be condemned. Rather, it is my hope that I have constructed a way by which imagist poetry can be read free of the assumptions of imagist theory, and through which the poetry can be seen for what it is: a relatively consistent manner with identifiable conventions and effects. In a sense, then, my aim is to salvage this poetry for those who, like myself, find its theoretical premises unconvincing. Both theory and practice are relevant to this study because it is the critical and creative dilemma posed by the theory which enables us to account for why the imagists wrote in the manner that they did. At some point, of course, it ought to be possible—and it would certainly be desirable—to discuss imagist poems without at the same time arguing the pros and cons of the imagist manifestos, without, that is, being polemical. This point is not reached in this work, however, because it is an attempt to account for the imagists' technical choices as well as to describe them.

As a further word of caution, let me add that any discussion of imagism must imply a stance toward the characteristic poetic procedures and assumptions of the present day. While imagism is notoriously narrow to some critics and poets writing today, to others it signifies the beginning of a continuing struggle for poetic purity. In such an atmosphere, it is difficult not to be controversial. I will have occasion to point to a few of the implications of this study for contemporary poetics and criticism, but, insofar as imagism itself was influential in creating some of these controversies, a full study of these implications seems to require that a preliminary treatment of the movement be constrained by historical limits. This is why I do not enter here into the debate of certain critical questions especially popular in recent years, even though my arguments often depend on my taking stances relative to such questions. For instance, I will depend on assumptions about the relationship between the reader and the text which are, in some circles, currently at issue. My reader-oriented approach, deriving as it does from the rhetorical tradition, should not be confused with the recent fashion for "reader-response" criticism, which depends on very different assumptions about intention and interpretation from those that I have appealed to. Likewise, my analysis of rhetorical structure should not be confused with one or another form of "structuralism," even though it is, I hope, informed by aspects of it. But again, my purpose here, in the context of the historical movement of imagism, is not to justify my assumptions in relation to any or all on-going critical controversies. Rather, because this is a study from a particular point of view, it is to state my assumptions as clearly as possible and to apply them to the specific issues the imagists themselves argued.

Since any critical study of imagism will naturally bring to mind the attacks made by Yvor Winters against this school of poets, I think it is appropriate to mention some ways in which this study departs from Winters', lest the whole affair seem to be the disinterment of a quarrel long dead and best left that way. One difference is that Winters often condemned the imagists' poetry as inept because of the ineptness he found in their ideas about poetry. But, more importantly, Winters' attacks derive from poetic values which I do not share. I do not, for instance, view poetry as "a technique of contemplation" as Winters did, particularly because Winters meant by this that the poet's "communication is first of all with himself." I would question the validity of this statement as a useful principle, even as I shall come to question similar statements by the imagists themselves. This conception of the function of poetry, in fact, resembles that of the imagists to such a degree that Winters may be said to have been in substantial agreement with them. His attacks, at this distance, seem to have been directed more at imagism's incompleteness than its inconsistency. This is especially evident in his treatment of "the mechanics of the poetic image," for which he adopted not only the doctrine of imagism but also its vocabulary. He defined the image, for example, as "a fusion of sense perceptions" which "presents the emotion; that is, the emotion is seen in the concrete and acts directly, without the aid of thought." It is clear that Winters considered the image, so defined, to be one of the functions of poetry, and he considered imagism to have failed to provide a comprehensive theory of its other functions, and so he supplemented it with a theory of the "anti-image."[1] But Winters' reasons are not, therefore, mine. I shall have occasion to refer to some of Winters' specific arguments about imagist theory, but I do not wish the reader to identify the whole of his outlook with my own.

The theme of this study is rhetoric, both my sense of the term and the imagists', the ways in which our senses are alike and how they differ. To avoid confusion on this score, I ought to point out initially that I have chosen this word *rhetoric*, in lieu of some other, because when it occurs in the writings of the imagists it represents a focal point for their theoretical reforms and when it appears in some modern criticism it similarly focuses many concepts which I have adopted as a critical perspective. Neither use of the term may accord with "rhetoric" in a classical or even in some preferred modern sense. Thus, if I argue that the poetry of the imagists is rhetorical, despite their claims to the contrary, I do not wish to quibble over what rhetoric *really* is. I wish to show only that the work of the imagists has certain features which make it what it is, and the argument over rhetoric provides a suitable locus for the discussion of the choice of these features in relation to the demands of the theory. This will entail, of course, a position on the question of whether the phrase "the rhetoric of poetry" is a contradiction in terms, as some think. If, as Elder Olson has put it, "we have never quite shaken off the rhetorical view of poetry,"[2] it is not because many poets and critics have not tried. But what none of the various anti-rhetorical theories of poetry have succeeded in doing is to rid poetry of its readers, and it is from the reader's point of view, as I shall argue in detail, that rhetoric emerges. When they do succeed, of course, the need to argue about such matters will have passed.

Unless otherwise noted, the poems I have chosen for analysis have been taken from the collections of imagist poetry listed in the first section of the bibliography: the four original imagist anthologies and the three subsequent collections of imagist verse. This exclusive use of anthologies explicitly labeled "imagist" is more arbitrary than it may seem, not only because the latter-day editors have included poems not in the original anthologies or journals, but also because the original collections themselves were put together for as many political reasons as poetic ones. In selecting examples from these collections, I have tried to maintain a sense of "normal imagism," if you will, which takes in what seems to have been the range of imagist expression but which excludes even certain poems in the original collections from consideration. Because the interest here is on the imagist mode, rather than on the achievement of individual imagist poets, I have not chosen examples from separate collections by members of the group, and I have sought to represent its lesser-known members as well as its better-known. For this same reason, I have not differentiated between the best imagist poems, which ought to outlast the dogma of imagism, and the worst, which will, when the time comes, be forgotten with it. Should many of the poems I cite here strike the reader as lamentably bad, perhaps a comparison with the magazine verse of more recent movements could at least provide an occasion to meditate on the idea of progress in the arts.

The list of those who have supported me in this project must begin with my wife, who knows without my thanking her here what thanks I would still owe. Among the teachers and colleagues to whom I owe debts of gratitude, direct and indirect, are William J. Brandt, N. Terence Busch, Seymour Chatman, Thomas Conley, Richard Filloy, Lawrence D. Green, Josephine Miles, L. Bart Queary, Arthur Quinn, Laurie Saunders, and Johanna Von Gottfried. I am grateful for the specific advice I have received from Monroe C. Beardsley, Robert Bloom, Edward P. J. Corbett, Ian Fletcher, Suzanne Juhasz, Thomas O. Sloane, and Ernest Waugh, who have read and commented on earlier versions of this study. To Leonard Nathan, for his continuous inspiration, encouragement, and criticism, I owe very special thanks. Having failed to do justice to the ideas I owe to all of these, I continue to trust in their generosity of mind.

This work has been made easier, if not better, by financial assistance from the following sources, for which I am grateful: the Graduate Division of the University of California, Berkeley; the Faculty Development Fund of Golden Gate University; and the Provost's Research Fund of Arizona State University.

In the Arresting Eye

Chapter One

THEORIES

The apparition of these faces
in a crowd
—Ezra Pound

Perspectives

In defense of imagist poetics, Ezra Pound maintained that "the 'image' is the furthest possible remove from rhetoric."[1] The present study is an attempt to measure that distance. How far is "the furthest possible remove?" One answer is that "image" and "rhetoric" are mutually exclusive categories and the distance between them is therefore immeasurable. The imagists themselves, in their theoretical pronouncements, held such a view. It will be my intention to show, however, that the distance separating the image and rhetoric is not very far, and indeed, that a great distance is not possible.

Such an assessment hinges on a general and perplexing problem: To what extent is it necessary to accept the theory in order to read the poetry? Put another way, it is a problem of perspective. Does the poetry make sense only if one approaches it from the point of view defined by the theory out of which it was written? If that theory proves to be inconsistent or fallacious, is it legitimate to approach the poetry from some other perspective?

The problems addressed in this study emerge from the dislocation of two perspectives: that of imagist theory and that of the uninitiated reader of imagist poetry. The reader's perspective is defined by assumptions about poetry in general; the perspective of the theory is defined by the poets' own assumptions about imagism in particular. The two perspectives happen to be at odds because the theory of imagism holds as one of its basic assumptions that imagist poetry is unique—capable, that is, of effects which other kinds of poetry are not. Such an assumption requires the reader to adopt a perspective toward imagist poetry which he would not adopt toward other sorts of poetry, and this implies the necessity of prior knowledge and acceptance of the theory on the part of the reader.

My study is motivated, then, by the observation, which I intend to support in several ways, that imagist theory is inadequate to account for the reader's actual experience of the imagist poem. It challenges, therefore, the assumption of imagism's uniqueness, by bringing to light certain effects which imagism shares with poetry in general. Even though the perspective I have chosen is contrary to the perspective defined by imagist theory, it permits these effects to be isolated. The many reasons for adopting this perspective will emerge in the course of the analyses to follow, both of the theory and of the poetry. But something about the perspective of the reader, as opposed to that of the imagist theorist, must be said initially.

My conclusions follow from a minimal assumption about poetry: A poem, like other sorts of discourse, has means by which it controls the reader's responses. This is not an extreme condition, since it does not necessarily commit one to the view that poetry uses the same means as other modes of discourse, nor that it necessarily employs them toward the same ends. It merely requires that a poem be considered as a creation which fulfills its end in the mind of the reader rather than in the poet or on the page as an inert object without an active perceiver. Nor does this condition require that a poem fulfill its end by communicating "meaning," so long as it is understood that communication can, and in poetry frequently does, include the creation of emotional experience. I will consider it axiomatic that there is an inevitable relationship between the *end* of poetry as an effect felt *by the reader* and the *means* by which that effect is controlled *in the poem*,[2] in spite of the fact that language does not permit an absolute control over the process.

One might say that the means of discourse are consistently

necessary *because* absolute control over the functions of language is not possible, considering that language is a symbolic, not a mathematically precise, activity. The sorts of means I am referring to are not to be found in the words themselves, in isolation, but in the functional ways in which words can be arranged to control a reader's experience of them. If words were mediators of undistorted reality—as the imagists seem to have conceived of them—then no such means would be needed. One of the assumptions of imagism, as we shall see, is that if the reader is given a reality as absolute as any object, no means of controlling the reader's response would be required. This assumption makes it necessary to ask whether the reader of imagist poems is expected to respond in other ways than the structures of language permit and require. If, as T. S. Eliot said, "language in a healthy state presents the object, is so close to the object that the two are identical,"[3] then it would follow, by the logic of imagism, that the reader's response is the result of an unmediated apprehension, one which the object itself could have produced as readily as the language of the poem. The fact that discourse brings with it a bundle of conventionally learned responses, at the level of its semantics, its syntax, and its structure, widens the gap between the word and the object. To the imagists this meant that language was in a state of ill health, and they sought a cure in arguing that poetry ought to rid language of these conventions.

The imagist poet wished to communicate emotion. Emotional experience which is stimulated in the poet by some occurrence in nature, when it is mediated by language and makes its way to the reader, is a reenactment one step removed, necessarily, for the reader has not the same stimulus before him, but a representation of it: its illusion. Although language provides efficient means of creating emotion in a reader, the means of language are not the same as the means of nature. Reality in language is always different from reality in nature; the literary process we call realism (of which imagism is one kind) is a process by which the experiences of nature are re-created by special *strategies* of language. If they are not the same experiences, the strategies of language have the power to make the reader ignore the difference in the process of experiencing them. To seem realistic is not to reproduce reality, though if an artist succeeds, by one means or another, we are made to put aside the distinction momentarily. If criticism focuses on the strategies of language, then, it can help us to understand this process.

From speculations of this sort, to which I shall have occasion to return, emerge two sorts of questions about the means of imagist poetry. One might ask, if the imagists desired not the illusion of the emotion but the emotion itself, what means did they consider necessary and sufficient to capture this direct apprehension in language? I shall attempt to answer this question by analyzing the imagists' theories. But imposing itself on this analysis must be the assumption which I have just put forward, from the reader's point of view, that although they desired to create this emotion by presenting the reader with the source of the emotion in "things," they are prevented by the nature of language as a discursive medium from achieving anything but its illusion. The second question, then, deals with the means that the imagists were in fact compelled to use for achieving the effect of this illusion. Naturally, to achieve the effect successfully is to use those means which language makes available to *convince* the reader of the reality. These means I shall call "the rhetoric of imagism."

I take the word *rhetoric* in this context from a suggestive passage in Wallace Stevens' *The Necessary Angel*: "There is always an analogy between nature and the imagination, and possibly poetry is merely the strange rhetoric of that parallel: a rhetoric in which the feeling of one man is communicated to another in words of the exquisite appositeness that takes away all their verbality." This "strange rhetoric" refers to the means, then, of achieving the illusion that words become "so close to the object that the two are identical." The imagists considered the image to be the means by which the reality of this transformation is accomplished, as we shall see. Stevens' view, here, is that the worlds of imagination and nature are parallel, but discrete. It might be contrasted to a view expressed by William Butler Yeats, for whom the two worlds are not assumed to be parallel, but correspondent. Yeats was said to have achieved a "realistic homology of mental images and physical things," when he wrote in his *Per Amica Silentia Lunae*, "If all our mental images no less than apparitions (and I see no reason to distinguish) are forms existing in the general vehicle of Anima Mundi and mirrored in our particular vehicle, many crooked things are made straight." "Crooked things" might be said to be those by which one is merely persuaded of the identity of mental images and physical things, and "straight things" the embodiment of their identity. The latter was the stated goal of imagism, which relied no less on metaphysics for its reasons. Yeats, significantly, defined rhetoric as "the will trying to do the work of the imagination."[4]

The imagists agreed with Yeats. They were committed to the view that rhetoric was at odds with the practice of poetry, and that it signified the failure of the imagination and the image. They desired, once and for all, to rid poetry of rhetoric, echoing the claim of Paul Verlaine that the goal of pure poetry was, quite simply, "to take rhetoric and wring its neck."[5] The image represented poetry purged of rhetoric.

I shall take up the question of the image as a rhetorical device in Chapter Three, the first of three chapters discussing the techniques that the imagists employed to create the effects they desired. I wish to turn now to the poetics of imagism, to discover what the imagists thought poetry should be. The stage will then be set for a discussion, in Chapter Two, of why they thought it was "rhetoric," specifically, that must be avoided in this ideal poetry.

Imagism: Theory and Contexts

The local history of the imagist movement is readily available, so I will not treat it at length, nor for any other reason than to provide some necessary background for this study. The years 1909–1917 roughly circumscribe the period during which a movement that called itself imagism was an active voice in English poetics. The first reference to "Les Imagistes" in print was made by Ezra Pound when, in 1912, he included "The Complete Poetical Works of T. E. Hulme" in his own volume *Ripostes*. Hulme's five poems were prefaced by Pound's remarks about a "forgotten school of 1909," "a school of Images," referring to a group of poets which had met formally under Hulme's auspices beginning in 1908, and which Pound himself joined when Hulme reorganized the club with F. S. Flint in 1909. Members of this "poets' club" were united in their "dissatisfaction with poetry as it was then written,"[6] and—encouraged perhaps by the knowledge that they were the hard core of a literary avant garde—they brought the full power of their intellectual resources to bear in finding new ways to write. Whatever the vagaries of their personal and political relations, Hulme's interest in aesthetics, Flint's bohemian devotion to the French symbolists and Japanese haiku, and Pound's knowledge of Romance languages provided early mutual reinforcement for an emerging poetics which was soon to be expressed in the form of prescriptions.

Despite his ambiguous preface to Hulme's poems, it is clear that Pound agreed with the premises that were developed by this group, although we have little record of their discussions. The same premises, presumably, are those which were articulated by Hulme in his later writings, some of them unfinished notes from years earlier. Hulme may be regarded as a principal theorist of the imagists, and Pound, in the period 1912–1914, although contributing original ideas, might be regarded as their chief publicist.[7] Through his association with Harriet Monroe, Pound launched his publicity campaign in January 1913 in *Poetry* magazine, using the label "Imagiste" to describe H. D., and introducing several imagist concepts in an essay, "Status Rerum." In March he contributed the manifesto, "A Few Don'ts by an Imagist."

The same issue included Flint's article "Imagisme," which speaks of the movement in the past tense, saying that its members "held a certain 'Doctrine of the Image,' which they had not committed to writing," and distinguishing them by their intolerance of any poetry not written by their rules, their earnestness, and their snobism. The movement spread to the pages of other literary magazines and associated itself with other influential figures, such as Remy de Gourmont. In 1914 Pound edited an anthology entitled *Des Imagistes*, made up of poems by Richard Aldington,

H. D., Pound, Flint, Ford Madox Ford (then Hueffer), William Carlos Williams, Skipwith Cannell, Amy Lowell, Allen Upward, John Cournos, and James Joyce. In the following years, three numbers of another anthology, *Some Imagist Poets*, appeared with poems by Aldington, H. D., John Gould Fletcher, Flint, D. H. Lawrence, and Lowell. Pound had nothing to do with these volumes, edited primarily by Lowell, and in fact he pressured to prevent the use of the earlier title. All was not unanimity in this school by then. Pound had previously launched "Vorticism" with Aldington, Ford, and Wyndham Lewis, expanding the original principles of imagism to apply to the arts in general, and he denounced the other faction as "Amygists."[8] There was considerable bickering over just what the principles were, and who had fathered them. Pound cited Ford as the source of imagist principles, and Ford concurred. Flint, in an article called "The History of Imagism," gave the credit for originality to Hulme. Aldington gave considerable credit to Flint himself, as did Robert Frost, who attended a few meetings, was admired by the group, but contributed nothing to the movement but his silence.[9]

A further *Imagist Anthology* was issued in 1930 with poems by nine out of a "total of thirteen writers who may possibly be considered *bona fide* Imagists,"[10] as an obvious gesture of nostalgia for a movement which the editors considered to have ended in 1917. This book did not intend to rejuvenate the movement, all of whose participants had matured in divergent ways, as the anthology itself demonstrates. Pound, of course, was then committed to the *Cantos*, signifying his own separation from these controversies, if not, perhaps, his abandonment of many of his early ideas about poetry.[11]

Such is the chronology of the name: imagism. The movement itself is replete with prose statements of policy, as well as five anthologies of verse in which to find representative products of those policies, all of which will serve as sources for this study. The revolution that imagism stood for, however, is more than a name, and if we are to consider the ideas for which the name stands, we have to stretch our chronological limits somewhat.[12] Clarification of the stances taken by the imagists may be found in sources which predate the movement itself. The question of direct lines of influence has been the subject of historians of the movement, and need not be mine here: Chronology is not so much an issue for this study as are shared assumptions about poetic technique. Imagism, then, is a name for a cluster of assumptions which are represented by the historical circle of imagists, but which are not confined to them.

The briefest description of the imagists' intention was provided by Herbert Read: "To cut the cackle." The cackle from which the group sought to free poetry was characterized as rigid, overblown, vague, sentimental, and unoriginal. The dissatisfactions of the group first emerged in the form of prescriptions in Pound's "A Few Don'ts," which can be summarized as an appeal for brevity ("Use no superfluous word"), concreteness ("Go in fear of abstractions"), objectivity ("Don't be viewy"), and unconventional verse forms ("Don't chop your stuff into separate iambs").[13] That they were put into the form of prescriptions is indicative of the reformist attitude which characterized imagist thought, and the imagists were viewed by a large part of the contemporary audience as a threat to poetry as they knew it.

As a result, it has been commonplace to argue that imagism represented a revolt against current and previous poetic practices, such as those of the Georgians, Victorians, or Pre-Raphaelites. Romanticism, in all of its manifestations, is considered to have been its primary target. The positions which the imagists shared with their romantic forefathers have for this reason often been overlooked, and these positions especially need emphasis. The survey of imagist principles which follows will proceed from a discussion of the metaphysics out of which imagism emerged, to its theory of the evolution of metaphor and the romantic heritage of such ideas as the ideogrammic method, the objectivity of the poet, and the poet's relation to the audience.

T. E. Hulme was a self-described antiromantic. He proclaimed the dawning of a new classicism, which, although it harked back to the spirit of such writers as Catullus and Pope, was not imitative of them. He thought of his classicism as a modern manifestation of the same motives as the classical poets', and for this reason he wished the modern poet to invent wholly new forms. In order to understand his conviction that the new poetry should be classic in spirit, yet altogether new, we must initially consider how it is rooted in a theory of language and art which Hulme derived chiefly from the French philosopher Henri Bergson, although Hulme's study of Remy de Gourmont, Jules de Gaultier, Georges Sorel, and Theodule Ribot certainly confirmed aspects of this theory. Hulme first met Bergson in 1907 and readily acquired a Bergsonian point of view. He translated the philosopher's *An Introduction to Metaphysics* in 1912 with the authorization and help of the author.[14] Hulme's own writings were attempts to make this philosophy more available to English audiences, and to extend it, largely into aesthetics.

In Hulme's best-known essay, "Romanticism and Classicism," probably composed in 1913 or 1914, we can see precisely how his Bergsonianism informs his poetics. Hulme gave the reasons that made him think the romantic movement was nearing its end: "The first lies in the nature of any convention or tradition in art. A particular convention or attitude in art has a strict analogy to the phenomena of organic life. It grows old and decays. It has a definite period of life and must die. All the possible tunes get played on it and then it is exhausted; moreover, its best period is its youngest." Hulme considered the romantic movement to have ground out in the Victorian era and the nineties because it had reached the point where the old conventions had been used up, and thus lacked the power to express the poet's feelings. This is a strict application of the dualistic metaphysics of Bergson. Convention corresponds to the first of two modes of perception which Bergson postulated in his *Introduction to Metaphysics*, the analytic and the intuitive. Elsewhere, he called them the "extensive" and the "intensive manifolds," terms which Hulme preferred in describing these perceptual operations. These two "ways of knowing" lead to "relative" or "absolute" perceptions, respectively. The analytic point of view "is to express a thing as a function of something else. All analysis is thus a translation, a development into symbols." Intuition, on the other hand, Bergson defined as "the kind of *intellectual sympathy* by which one places oneself within an object in order to coincide with what is unique in it,"[15] and thus it is by means of intuition alone that one can view a thing as other than a translation, as itself. He called, in his essay, for a method of speculation which would employ intuition to arrive at a realization of this "absolute" perception of the external world. This, for Bergson, was the way to truth. What for Bergson was a proper method of thought became for Hulme a proper method of poetic creation, a method which he associated with classicism.

Hulme stressed repeatedly the necessity for the poet to get at the way things "really are" as opposed to the way we are accustomed to perceive them by analytic habits of mind, that is, by conventional modes of thought. He considered the analytic faculty to result from training, whereas the intuitive is necessarily spontaneous. He said, in "Romanticism and Classicism," that "there are then two things to distinguish, first the particular faculty of the mind to see things as they really are, and apart from the conventional ways in which you have been trained to see them." Conventional means of perception, and expression, do not allow one to penetrate into the subject, as Bergson put it, because analytic perception confines itself to the external, relational point of view, which is how "we have been trained to see." In Coleridgean terms, according to Hulme, the extensive manifold corresponds to "Imagination," the perception of abstract ideas as opposed to concrete things. This identification is possible because Bergson insisted that analysis must confine itself to relations, whereas the object of the intuitive faculty is "things," in and of themselves. Things, in turn, are the material of images. Thus, Hulme preferred "Fancy," defined by Coleridge as "the faculty for bringing together images dissimilar in the main by some one point or more of likeness distinguished."[16] Hulme may have responded favorably to the word *images* in Coleridge, while ignoring the relational aspect of his definition. This confusion in Hulme's mind, between the extensive manifold which distorts reality by being relational, and the intensive manifold which reveals reality because intuitive—but which is produced in poetry by the construction of analogies—is one which must confront us as we attempt to sort out the imagist argument. Coleridge clearly defined a process of comparison, which Hulme and Pound at times endorsed as the medium of the images and at other times condemned as a rhetorical convention.

Since the poetry inherited from previous generations was made up of habitual conventions, from Hulme's point of view, it no longer suited the process of expressing the true nature of things, and had to be refashioned for this purpose. This had to be done along the lines suggested by Coleridge, by bringing dissimilar images together. Images were the record of the "thing" as perceived by the poet; they were "the very essence of an intuitive language." Metaphor, in order to take its place in this metaphysic, had to be constructed in some manner which would bring this spontaneous, intensive perception of reality to the surface. The manner of this construction had to be new, unconventional. For Hulme, this meant that the creation of the image ought to reproduce the process of the evolution of metaphor in primitive language. "Poetry," he said, is "always the advance guard of language. The progress of language is the absorption of new analogies." He was convinced, after the popular philologists of the day, such as Otto Jespersen, that language originated as poetry, or as common words applied metaphorically to new experience and hence developing new meanings. New meanings were thought to be a direct result of the perceiver's apprehension of the "thing itself," but when language became conventional, through repeated use, it no longer functioned to record this apprehension. The new meanings themselves became common. Prose meaning, then, he considered to be a state of decay. He defined the language which we inherit from prose as "the relics of extravagant fancies and analogies of dead and forgotten poets," calling it a "museum" of dead metaphors.[17] He understood the metaphor to be the production of a wholly new idea based on an analogy between two things as perceived by the senses. Again, we may trace this concept to Bergson's metaphysics. In Hulme's translation, Bergson said:

> Many diverse images, borrowed from very different orders of things, may, by the convergence of their action, direct consciousness to the precise point where there is a certain intuition to be seized. By choosing images as dissimilar as possible, we shall prevent any one of them

from usurping the place of intuition it is intended to call up, since it would then be driven away at once by its rivals. By providing that, in spite of their differences of aspect, they all require from the mind the same kind of attention, and in some sort the same degree of tension, we shall gradually accustom consciousness to a particular and clearly-defined disposition—that precisely which it must adopt in order to appear to itself as it really is, without any veil.[18]

This passage clearly shows why the theory of the poetic image developed from Hulme's thinking about Bergson necessitates *two* images, at least: whereas a single image is but a picture of a thing, it is the "convergence" of images which is thought to stimulate intuitive perception, so long, that is, as the converging images are "borrowed from very different orders of things." The reason that these images must be "as dissimilar as possible" is apparently to counteract the tendency of the mind to see one of them in terms of the other, in which case one image would take precedence and the intuition would be diluted by the conventional operations of comparison. Bergson referred to this poetic process as "to proceed by . . . juxtaposition," a phrase echoed by Pound in his defense of the "ideogrammic method," or the fusion of two images into one which he called "super-position." Fletcher's term for the presentation of two such images was "the unrelated method." Such juxtapositions by whatever name resulted in what Hulme called "a visual chord." [19]

The image was more than a means of expressing the true nature of things, then; it was a means of discovering it. Hulme put it this way: "Thought," he said, "is the joining together of new analogies, and so inspiration is a matter of accidentally seen analogy or unlooked-for resemblance." The process of recording images was said to be accidental because poetic inspiration must begin in sense perception. Hulme, for example, recorded in his notebook the sort of observation which might lead to an imagist poem: "The two tarts walking along Picadilly on tiptoe, going home, with hat on back of head. Worry until could find the exact model analogy that will reproduce the extraordinary effect they produce. Could be done at once by an artist in a blur." To be a creative artist, for Hulme, it is "necessary to get as large as possible change in sense impressions, cf. looking in shop windows. . . . The more change of shapes and sights there is the more chance of inspiration."[20] Pound's own account of how he came to write his poem "In a Station of the Metro," though perhaps less voyeuristic than Hulme's, is identical in form:

> Three years ago in Paris I got out of a "metro" train at La Concorde, and saw suddenly a beautiful face, and then another and another, and then a beautiful child's face, and then another beautiful woman, and I tried all day to find words for what this had meant to me, and I could not find any words that seemed to me worthy, or as lovely as that sudden emotion. And that evening . . . I found, suddenly, the expression. I do not mean that I found words, but there came an equation . . . not in speech, but in little splotches of color.[21]

Pound went on to say that if he were to paint this image he would produce a "non-representative" painting such as advocated by Kandinsky in *Ueber das Geistige in der Kunst*, similar, perhaps, to Hulme's "blur." The nonrepresentative painting is a suitable analogy because the image so produced was not intended to be a representation, it seems, but an "equation" for an emotion, made out of separate images. (The imagists used the word *image* indiscriminately to refer to both the single descriptive phrase and the result of the combination of two such phrases.)

In order to produce this image, the intuitive faculty must escape the temporal "flux," which, according to Bergson, always operated to distort perception by showing everything to us in relation to something else, in constant action. Our habit of perceiving things in "certain fixed ways" results from our perceiving them in time, in other words, and we are thereby prevented from entering into "intellectual sympathy" with things in an absolute sense. To penetrate this flux, then, one has to isolate the objects of perception in time. Hulme wrote, after Bergson, that "the creative activity of the artist is only necessary because of the limitations placed on internal and external perception by the necessities of action. If we could break through the veil which action interposes, if we could come into direct contact with sense and consciousness, art would be useless and unnecessary. Our eyes, aided by memory, would carve out in space and fix in time the most inimitable of pictures."[22] Hulme's rationale for the function of art is echoed in Pound's criteria for the poetic image, the definition of which runs: "An 'Image' is that which presents an intellectual and emotional complex in an instant of time. . . . It is the presentation of such a 'complex' instantaneously which gives that sense of sudden liberation; that sense of freedom from time limits and space limits; that sense of sudden growth, which we experience in the presence of the greatest works of art."[23] The definition repeats the Hulme/ Bergson principle that art must free us from the limitations of time, and to free us from time is to stop it "in an instant." It was the necessity to escape action that drew the imagists to the pictorial arts for their model of presentation. Things are apprehended "instantly" through vision, and vision thus became the principal sense to which this poetry must appeal. Hulme considered that the visual sense alone could make the poem achieve the liberation which both he and Pound desired. "This new verse," wrote Hulme, "appeals to the eye rather than to the ear. It has to mould images, a kind of spiritual clay, into definite shapes. The material . . . is image and not sound. It builds up a plastic image which it hands over to the reader, whereas the old art endeavoured always to influence him."[24]

Because of Pound's well-schooled ear, his obvious interest in prosody, it is reasonable to think that he would have found Hulme's rejection of sound in poetry repugnant. He did, after all, offer the traditional definition of poetry as "a composition of words set to music" and claim that "most other definitions of it are indefensible." When Pound spoke of phanopoeia, the "casting of images upon the visual imagination," as a *kind* of poetry, he did not mean that such poetry will lack the property of melopoeia, the "musical property" of words. He found in the visual sense a convenient metaphor, however, for describing the effect which he thought all art to have on the perceiver, frequently using the term *primary pigment* to describe the "point of maximum energy" in the various arts, or their most basic property: "Every concept, every emotion presents itself to the vivid consciousness in some primary form. It belongs to the art of this form. If sound, to music; if formed words, to literature; the image, to poetry." By saying that the image is the primary pigment of poetry, Pound used vision as his metaphor for the direct apprehension of emotion in poetry. He might have disagreed with Hulme, then, about poetry's exclusive appeal to the eye, but he shared with Hulme the visual metaphor as a means of expressing the distinction between *influencing* the reader and *handing over* the image directly. This is the meaning of the term *presents* in his definition. Pound is no less Bergsonian for denying that poetry is exclusively visual, if we stress that the image was meant to occur instantaneously, freeing one from the limitations that time imposes on perception. When Pound said that "an *image*, in our sense, is real because we know it directly," he was in substantial agreement with Hulme's statement that poetry "is not a counter language, but a visual, concrete one. It is a compromise for a language of intuition which would hand over sensations bodily. It always endeavours to arrest you, and make you continuously see a physical thing, to prevent you gliding through an abstract process." The agreement lies in an appeal to the immediacy of the experience by which reality is known, directly. "The function of art," said Pound, "is to strengthen the perceptive faculties and free them from encumbrance, such encumbrances, for instance, as set moods, set ideas, conventions." Freed from such encumbrances, one is able to have experiences induced by "the inevitable laws of nature." [25]

The critic Robert Langbaum has shown, in another context, that one of the principal characteristics of romanticism, a nearly constant essential in poetic theory since the Enlightenment, is "the doctrine that the imaginative apprehension gained through immediate experience is primary and certain, whereas the analytic reflection that follows is secondary and problematical." [26] In spite of Hulme's antiromantic stance, it is clear that the concepts which he contributed to the imagist movement derive from this tradition. Indeed, these same concepts provide the basis of Shelley's argument in "A Defence of Poetry." Shelley begins with a distinction between reason and imagination which corresponds to the Hulme/Bergson categories: reason operates by means of analysis, the "enumeration of quantities already known," while imagination is synthesis, "the perception of the values of those qualities." In

Shelley, poetry is defined as "the expression of the imagination," and it is "connate with the origin of man." That is, in Shelley as in Hulme, primitive man spoke poetry, but because social man is "determined to action," the originally vital metaphors die, they "become, through time, signs for portions or classes of thoughts instead of pictures of integral thoughts." But the "reflected image" of those original impressions can be restored by poets whose language "marks the before unapprehended relations of things." According to Shelley, the poet's "words unveil the permanent analogy of things by images which participate in the life of truth." Hulme's own poetic exactly corresponds, and repeats the same key words, despite the fact that he viewed romanticism and the "cosmic" poets-it fostered as the antithesis of what he wanted poetry to become.[27]

Murray Krieger has also given abundant evidence that Hulme, as an imagist, was "battling romanticism with the tools furnished him by romanticism," in the sense that the imagist conception of intuition consistently proclaims the romantic poet's ideals of expressionism and organicism. The insistence that the poet can catch a glimpse of the reality of nature by escaping the temporal flux and can present his image in such a way that the reader will be similarly freed, is another way in which imagism shared a romantic ideal. The imagist's "instant of time" resembles Wordsworth's "spots of time," or Pater's "the exquisite moment." Pater was nearer that generation which the imagists rejected for having exhausted the resources of its forms, and for having produced, consequently, conventional verse. But the intention of that generation, insofar as Pater was its spokesman, was imagistic: "Every moment," wrote Pater in *The Renaissance*, "some form grows perfect in hand or face; some tone on the hills or the sea is choicer than the rest; some mood of passion or intellectual insight is irresistably real . . . *for that moment only*." Like Hulme, he went on to say that the formulation of "stereo-typed" ways of perception gives a "roughness" to the eye, making the ecstasy of such moments impossible, just as Coleridge had made the identification of an object in its original concreteness depend on lifting "the film of familiarity."[28]

The expression of this intense moment of truth, resulting from unveiling the faculty of perception, therefore, links the imagists not only with romantics such as Shelley or even Blake, but also with the more conservative aestheticists of the Victorian generation, against whom they were in ostensible revolt. Hulme and Pater were in agreement that poetry was the result of a unique disposition to see nature "from the inside," as Hulme said, or, in Pater's words, "an intimate consciousness of the expression of natural things, which weighs, listens, penetrates, where the earlier mind passed roughly by." Pater ascribed this "intimate consciousness" to Wordsworth, whose statement of intention in the "Preface" to *Lyrical Ballads* prefigures a number of imagist concepts: "The principal object, then, proposed in these Poems was to choose incidents and situations from common life . . . and, above all, to make these incidents and situations interesting by tracing in them, truly though not ostentatiously, the primary laws of our nature: chiefly, as far as regards the manner in which we associate ideas in a state of excitement." Even though Hulme considered himself antiromantic in expressing similar ends, adding to them only the machinery of a metaphysics of metaphor, Pound reluctantly confessed that Wordsworth had been an ally, calling him "a silly old sheep with a genius, an unquestionable genius, for imagisme, for a presentation of natural detail." [29] His reluctance to say the same for the poetry of the Victorians was not due to any fundamental disagreement about the ends of poetry as perception of an exquisite moment, but to the ostentatiousness (to borrow Wordsworth's term) of their versification, the technical matters that Pound and Hulme associated with rhetoric and which I shall discuss briefly in the next chapter.

The same qualities which would make Pound recognize a fellow traveler in Wordsworth, despite his reservations, drew the imagists to models from the Orient, to the Chinese ideogram and the Japanese haiku. The metaphysics of Bergson provided a conceptual model from which imagism could be argued, but such poetic practices as these confirmed the validity of the model, and could be imitated. In the early days of the poet's club, Hulme and Flint were writing imitation haiku and tanka, and they introduced them to Pound as models for pictorial presentation.[30] In a recollection of his own, later, association with the imagists, Fletcher recorded the conditions which made poetry from the Orient, in European translations, seem so appealing. "In common with all the advanced poetry writers of the period," he wrote, "I was in full revolt from the Victorians. . . . It seemed to me that all English poets, from Shelley to Wordsworth onward, had tried too hard to make poetry teach something, preach something, bear the abstract connotation of a general moral lesson—when the real business of poetry was to state, and state concretely, just what had moved the poet, and to leave the reader to draw his own conclusions." Fletcher credited the Chinese poets with going about this real business of poetry: concrete statement with no moral lesson. He included a list of titles that suggests that in the two decades preceding imagism a significant revival of interest in Oriental literature was taking place, and that the need for examples outside the romantic tradition was felt by others besides the imagists. But the specific conditions of concreteness, emotional expression, conciseness, and pictorial quality which this verse seemed to possess for its translators attracted the imagists by predisposition. Fletcher equated the Bergsonian ideal of "intellectual sympathy" with the practice of the Chinese poets by saying that they "had used their imaginations to identify themselves with the objects they wrote about." The Oriental poem, Fletcher said, succeeded in producing "an objective equivalent in words to the object" actually seen.[31]

These attractions gained the benefit of scholarly authority when, in 1913, Pound came into possession of the manuscript of Ernest Fenollosa's essay, "The Chinese Written Character as a Medium for Poetry," which he edited for publication and used as a basis for many of his later statements in defense of imagistic methods. Fenollosa's ideas were naturally attractive to the imagists, not only because they verified the metaphysics that seemed to generate the Chinese and Japanese poems which the imagists had been imitating, but because they filled in a gap left by the Bergsonian model. But in another sense, Fenollosa's ideas clearly deny a basic Bergsonian principle, with the result that the imagists were faced with a contradiction they never adequately accounted for, nor even seemed to acknowledge.

Fenollosa's essay confirmed the poetics of imagism in a number of ways. In it he argued that the Chinese ideogram developed out of a primitive perception of relations between natural objects, *i.e.* that it was metaphorical, in Hulme's sense of being an intuitive construct. Just as Hulme had proposed that language decays when such metaphors no longer communicate this intuition, Fenollosa said that "a late stage of decay is arrested and embalmed in the dictionary." In English, this process of decay was continual, as metaphors become conventional and lose their power to "appeal to emotions with the charm of direct impression, flashing through regions where the intellect can only grope." Fenollosa said that poetry must retain this power. The advantage of the ideogram as a poetic medium, then, was that its etymology was visibly present in its written form, and the root words which combined to create its direct appeal were perceptible in its present state. Fenollosa argued that in Chinese one could continue to see the original metaphor, "to watch this transformation going on," and that the ideogram never lost its natural origins through abstraction, as English did by becoming conventional. "Chinese notation," said Fenollosa, "is something much more than arbitrary symbols. It is based upon a vivid shorthand picture of the operations of nature. In the algebraic figure and in the spoken word there is no natural connection between thing and sign: all depends upon sheer convention. But the Chinese method follows natural suggestion." The ideogram was indeed the paradigm of the image: it was assumed to be natural rather than conventional, a living metaphor which is "more than analogy, it is identity of structure"; it was therefore direct, visibly concrete; it appealed to the emotions by revealing nature. But how were these qualities to be translated into English?

Fenollosa provided an answer, but the imagists did not follow his specific advice, because it revealed that behind Fenollosa's poetic lay a fundamental contradiction of imagist metaphysics as derived from Bergson. Fenollosa held that the picture which an ideogram embodied was a representation of an *action*. In direct opposition to Bergson, Fenollosa said, "Perhaps we do not always sufficiently consider that thought is successive, not through some accident or weakness of our subjective operations but because the operations of nature are successive. The transferences of force from agent to object, which constitute natural phenomena, occupy time. Therefore, a reproduction of them in imagination requires the same temporal order." Rather than conceiving of the truth of nature as "things" distorted by the necessity of perceiving of them in the flux of action, Fenollosa considered that things in isolation prevent our perception of the reality of time in natural phenomena. "It is not so well known," Fenollosa wrote, "that the great number of these ideographic roots carry in them a *verbal idea of action*. It might be thought that a picture is naturally the picture of a *thing*, and that therefore the root ideas of Chinese are what grammar calls nouns." But he asserted instead that the ideogram provides a picture of a verb, and that "one superiority of verbal poetry as an art rests in its getting back to the fundamental reality of *time*." The effect of Fenollosa's study of the ideogram, therefore, was the assertion that the uniquely poetic form in English was necessarily the active, transitive sentence, which "brings language close to *things*," by a "strong reliance upon verbs."

How this conflicts with the principle of the instantaneous, processless image, which frees one from the limits of time, is obvious. What is not so obvious is that the imagists chose to ignore this basis of Fenollosa's claims because it forced one to conclude that English could not be suited for the production of images at all. Fenollosa was interested in the manipulation of syntax to produce the effect of time, whereas Hulme's poetic and Pound's definition of the image allowed no room for the operations of a poem to depend on its syntax. Insofar as syntax requires the manipulation of relations and the conventions of linear order for articulation, it would correspond to the extensive manifold, and thus, from Hulme's point of view, would be a hindrance to clear perception. For Fenollosa, the syntax of nature is that which the poet must perceive and imitate. Nevertheless, the pictorial quality of the ideogram, despite Fenollosa's actual arguments concerning its function, seemed to the imagists to be as close as language could come to *things* in themselves. Theirs was a poetry of nouns, despite Fenollosa's axiom that "a true noun, an isolated thing, does not exist in nature." [32]

Another aspect of Fenollosa's treatise, and of the available Oriental models—as Fletcher's account has already indicated—was that it cast the poet in the role of an objective observer. The Oriental poet was assumed to have no moral stance toward the things he observed; he did not editorialize. "Primitive men who created language agreed with science and not with logic," said Fenollosa, and so "poetry agrees with science and not with logic," as well. Logic signified abstract judgment but the Chinese mode of minute observation signified detachment and scientific neutrality. Pound literally undertook to make the poet a scientist, and objectivity therefore became a further requirement of imagist doctrine. The imagist poet was prevented from moralizing by his obligation to observe emotional phenomena and record them in concrete terms, as the ideogram was considered to do. "The serious artist," wrote Pound, "is scientific in that he presents the image of his desire," and thus "the arts provide the *data* for ethics." [33] Just as it is the biological scientist's duty to discover how men are the same, Pound argued, so it is the poet's duty to discover how they differ. The artist, as scientist of the emotions, merely records what he finds. He collects "data."

One of the ironies of the imagist perspective, which will become central to the discussion later in this study, is the conflict produced by this scientific stance on the one hand and the autonomy of the image on the other. By this I mean that the poet who is a collector of "data for *ethics*" must be presumed to feel an ultimate responsibility toward the improvement of human behavior. Pound even began his discussion of these matters with the statement that "it is obvious that the good of the greatest number cannot be attained until we know . . . of what that good must consist." He did not deny that knowledge of ethics is not an end in itself, but a means toward the end of ethical action. Yet, in the metaphysics of imagism lay the seeds of an autotelic standard for poetry, that it exists for its own sake. In the same discussion, for example, Pound stated quite emphatically that "art never asks anybody to do anything, or to think anything, or to be anything. It exists as the trees exist."[34] This is a rather final statement of *l'art pour l'art*, occasioned, we must conclude, by the necessity of the poet to remain objective, which requires the poet to "present" reality without accepting any responsibility to "influence" the reader.

The reason for failing to accept responsibility for influencing the reader is fairly obvious. The intuitive faculty, which allowed such glimpses of reality to be had, disallowed for them to be communicated, insofar as any means of communication, such as language, depends on conventions; and the existence of conventions is what was assumed to prevent the intuitive faculty from operating. The ideals of Fenollosa and the evolutionary view of the natural origin of metaphor depended on a condition of language imitating nature, and to an extent becoming nature. If poetic inspiration, furthermore, is a matter of accident, rather than a matter of intention, then the poet becomes a vehicle for nature's expression of itself and has no further understanding to transmit. The reader is simply on his own. Perhaps it was to such implications that William Butler Yeats was referring when he complained that "the only real Imagist was the Creator of the Garden of Eden."[35] At any rate, if the poet adopts the stance of the scientist, it suggests a desire not only to translate nature but also to understand it. If the nature at issue, furthermore, is the nature of human emotions and ethics, then it suggests also that the poet must desire to apply it to the human condition, to communicate it, to become an advocate for what he has discovered.

At the same time that it creates this conflict, however, the imagist argument paradoxically solves it. The analytical / intuitive dichotomy parallels a distinction in imagist theory between communication and *direct* communication, the former being the sort of relation a poet makes with a reader whom he wishes to influence by fulfilling the expected conventional forms of language, and the latter being that relation created by breaking such expectations and thereby removing perception's "veil." Hulme defined art as "a passionate desire for accuracy," and he defined "the essentially aesthetic emotion as the excitement generated by direct communication." He went on to explain that "ordinarily language communicates nothing of the freshness of things. As far as that quality goes we live separated from each other. The excitement of art comes from this rare and unique communication."[36] It is not necessary to abandon the aestheticism of Pound's statement that "art never asks anybody . . . to think anything," as long as one can distinguish a category called "direct communication" which is the result of this autotelic process, a process which does not, in other words, involve the *intention* to communicate and thus frees the poet from the obligation of using conventions because they are shared by the reader.

This paradox, which is perhaps what Hulme was referring to in calling poetry a "compromise" with language, and which therefore allows the poet to have it both ways, is a familiar one in the aesthetic theory of the generation prior to imagism. It is remindful of the answer given by A. C. Bradley, for instance, who had gone over some of the same ground in his Oxford lecture, "Poetry for Poetry's Sake." Bradley called poetry "a world unto itself," and yet he claimed that it provided the reader with "a succession of experiences." The middle position which he ultimately struck between the poem as an end in itself and the poem as a means to an effect in the reader prefigures the imagist ideal: the poem is an end in itself, but it cannot be cut off from life; it is, therefore, as Bradley said, an "analogue" of life. The following passage from Bradley's lecture clearly shows us the link between the imagist notion of "the thing itself" and those who came before: "What is the gist of Pater's teaching about style if it is not that in the end the one virtue of style is truth or adequacy; that the word, phrase, sentence, should express perfectly the writer's perception, feeling, image or thought; so that, as we read a descriptive phrase of Keats we exclaim, 'that is the thing itself'; so that, to quote Arnold, the words are 'symbols equivalent with the thing symbolized.'" The "direct communication" sought by the imagists is the result of presenting "equations for the human emotions," to use Pound's terms, through an analog in nature, or as Ford said, "rendering the facts of life without comment and in exact language."[37] It can be justified only if the reader is expected to react to the thing in the poem as if it were "the thing itself."

The question of the image as an efficient means of creating such moments of direct communication, as well as the assumptions involved in using images as "data for ethics," will concern us at several points as we attempt to move from imagist theory to a perspective which accounts for the reader's experience of imagist poems. At this point, however, it is enough to ask how such a theory can be expected to work. The "analog" of nature, however accurate an image may seem, must be ambiguous in a way that nature itself is not. If it is the artist's task to "present" the precise correlative of an emotional state through this analog, then it seems that in order for direct communication to result the reader is presumed to be able to reverse the intuitive process, to feel the emotion upon taking in the image. Is this process possible? Is it possible, that is, to get beyond the point of exclaiming, with Bradley, "that is the thing itself"? The condition that seems to make it possible is that nature and human emotions are precisely and unambiguously correspondent, which makes the poet's task one of creating a language that shares this correspondence. The imagists' apparent faith that this correspondence exists seems to be another unacknowledged inheritance from the romantic tradition. Here, for example, is Pater's assessment of Wordsworth's pantheism, seen through the lens of his own:

> And so it came about that this sense of a life in natural objects, which in most poetry is but a rhetorical artifice, is with Wordsworth the assertion of what for him is almost literal fact. To him every natural object seemed to possess more or less of a moral or spiritual life, to be capable of a companionship with man, full of expression, of inexplicable affinities. . . . It was like a "survival" . . . of that primitive condition, which some philosophers have traced to the general history of human culture, wherein all outward objects alike . . . were believed to be endowed with animation and the world was "full of souls." [38]

Although never stating their faith so boldly, the imagists depended on a connection between natural objects and emotions as the mechanism which makes direct communication of emotion through images work, as we shall see in greater detail later, just as they held onto the related conviction that art which fails to contact this level of affinity is "but a rhetorical artifice." The need to create a language which shared in this affinity, a metaphorical language such as was spoken intuitively by those who maintained a "primitive" vision of this affinity, occasioned the antirhetorical impulses of imagist theory. The fact that the imagists could hold, with Pound, that "a poem is supposed to present the truth of passion,"[39] and yet their failure to generalize about what this truth is, or what ethical principles derive from the poet's data, seems to indicate their faith that such truths and such principles were self-evident.

This self-evident correspondence between nature and emotion furnishes a point of reference from which to discuss the relation between imagism and certain ideas from the French symbolist movement. The immediate influence was probably through a popular study of symbolism by Arthur Symons, *The Symbolist Movement in Literature*, rather than through a firsthand encounter; among the early imagists only Flint knew of the symbolist poets in the original. To a group of like-minded poets in England, the symbolists were no doubt attractive by virtue of their solidarity. This solidarity may have been more Symons' invention than a precise account of history, since Symons was intent on promulgating a theory of his own, under Yeats's influence,[40] a theory which in its basic premises resembles imagism more than does his treatment of any single French poet. It consisted of an overriding concern for a poetry which rendered the invisible world tangible through the purification of language, and the evocation of emotion, rather than the use of reason, to penetrate nature and express its mystical verities. Symons desired a poetry which could precisely render the spiritual landscape. This meant that "properly, there is no metaphor; the words say exactly what they mean; they become figurative, as we call it, in their insistence on being themselves fact." Pound later echoed Symons, it seems, in his claim that "the natural object is always the *adequate* symbol."[41] It was Symons' aim that the poet use language which transcended semantic functions, words which did not denote, but which were capable of embodying and evoking the perception itself. They shared the sense that language had to be changed before the poet could use it.

In summarizing the achievement of Stephen Mallarmé, Symons put the challenge to future poets, which the imagists took up. "It is," he said, "on the lines of that spiritualizing of the word, that perfecting of form in its capacity for allusion and suggestion, that *confidence in the eternal correspondences between the visible and the invisible universe . . .* that literature must now move, if it is in any sense to move forward." F. S. Flint defined the symbolist movement in terms which precisely relate the spiritualism of Symons to imagism, but which replace that spiritualism with psychology. "Ultimately," he said, "it was an attempt to evoke the subconscious element of life, to set vibrating the infinity within us, by the exquisite juxtaposition of images." Flint went on to draw an explicit parallel between the symbolists and Bergson, saying that the symbol, like the image, "attempts to give you an intuition of the reality itself and of the forces, vague to us, behind it, by a series of images which the imagination seizes and brings together in an effort to insert itself into and express that reality, and to evoke at the same time the infinity of which it is the culminating point in the present." [42]

What is generally left out of symbolism, however, in its redefinition as imagism via Bergson, is precisely the mystical, or spiritual, nature of poetry which Symons took to be the symbolist's achievement. Although Symons described Mallarmé as engaged in a "chimerical search after the virginity of language" (a search carried out equally by Hulme and Fenollosa), the imagists were less prone to include a magical explanation for the discovery. They parted company with the symbolists in being naturalists more than supernaturalists, psychologists rather than alchemists. Among the symbolists, Arthur Rimbaud, like Hulme later, thought of convention as the immediate source of the failure of the poetic impulse, but unlike Hulme he wanted to "invent new flowers, a new flesh, a new language." Hulme was content to stop at the creation of a new language, so that he could see those flowers that already existed, as long as he saw them *really*. The symbolists sought not only a transcendence of language, but a transcendence of nature as well. Language, therefore, was nearly irrelevant to the symbolists' motives, as Symons presents them. He shows us Verlaine, for example, taking the extreme position that the poet uses language in order to destroy it. Verlaine's chief regard for language was that it got in the way. He desired *romances sans parole*, or "songs almost without words, in which scarcely a sense of the interference of human speech remains."[43]

The imagists shared this distrust of language, although their intention was to purify rather than to destroy it. The fault of language, as Hulme saw it, was that it was all extensive manifold, and the sort of poetic expression he sought had to be carried out in a language made intensive. Hulme thought of the poet as struggling to compromise with "a large clumsy instrument," as he called language, like teaching tricks to a worm. He thought too that the poet could not find an entirely satisfactory way to communicate in language. "Language," he said, "only expresses the lowest common denominator of the emotions of one kind. It leaves out all the individuality of an emotion as it really exists and substitutes for it a kind of stock or type emotion. . . . As we not only express ourselves in words, but for the most part think also in them, it comes about that not only do we not express more than the impersonal element in emotion, but that we do not, as a matter of fact, perceive more." The imagist stance was more than an attempt to create a new language for the purpose of better perceiving and better communicating the nature of things and their relation to human emotions. It was an attempt to oppose the very nature of language, which was alien to those ends. It was alien precisely because, as an instrument for recording the uniqueness of each emotion, language, the only available medium for the poet, was doomed to failure by virtue of being communal. It was "common," as Hulme lamented, "to you, me and everybody."[44]

This distrust of the common language would not be warranted if it did not appear in the context of a conviction that poetry, as Hulme said, is "not for others, but for the poet." The distrust of language, that is, has its roots in a distrust of readers. Symons defined the symbolist stance toward the reader as "disinterestedness," saying that Mallarmé, for instance, "made neither intrusion upon nor concession to those who, after all, were not obliged to read him." The movement saw itself, according to Symons' report, as unwilling to condescend to the standards of readers who were not themselves spiritually in tune with the movement, and they did not "attempt to touch the popular heart," simply because the nature of the experiences they wrote about could "never be comprehended by the crowd." Pound shared enthusiastically in this dislike for the public; he bore no respect for the common reader. "One should make NO compromise with the public," he said. "Art begins only when one has ceased to react to the imbecilities of the multitude."[45]

Such statements are not in themselves, of course, any condemnation of the idea that the poet must write for an audience, as Hulme's statement that poetry is "not for others" might be. Pound's attitude toward the audience of imagist poems is perhaps better seen in his discussion of the relation between the health of the language that the poet inherits from others. He made it clear that if a poet is to succeed, he must change the very language of his audience. The function of poetry, he said

> has to do with maintaining the very cleanliness of the tools, the health of the very matter of thought itself. Save in the rare and limited instances of invention in the plastic arts, or in mathematics, the individual cannot think and communicate his thought, the governor and the legislator cannot act effectively or frame his laws, without words, and the solidity and validity of these words is in the care of the damned and despised *litterati*. When their work goes rotten—by which I do not mean when they express indecorous thoughts—but when their very medium, the very essence of their work, *the application of word to thing* goes rotten, i.e. becomes slushy and inexact, or excessive or bloated, the whole machinery of social and individual thought and order goes to pot.[46]

Pound thought himself to live in such an age, an age in which the imbecile multitude and the litterati—the public and the poet together—were equally culpable in allowing their language to go rotten, and they were therefore ill-disposed to be communicated to until their language could be cleansed. It was as if the purpose of imagism—"the application of word to thing"—was to execute this cleansing in order that others might be able to use the language to communicate in some other context. Like Hulme, Pound thought that language wears out with use, but the function of the poet was to keep it well, and so he called poets "conservators of the public speech." He wrote, "It has been the function of poets to new-mint the speech, to supply the vigorous terms of prose." Pound could assert an autotelic status for poetry, that "it exists as the trees exist," because he held that its function was not to communicate in any ordinary sense of the term, but to be responsible only to its own purity. He said, for instance, that "the conception of poetry as a 'pure art' in the sense in which I use the term, revived with Swinburne. From the puritanical revolt to Swinburne, poetry had been merely the vehicle . . . for transmitting thoughts, poetic or otherwise."[47] Thus, insofar as the existence of an audience assumes that the poet uses the language of that audience in order to say something to it, to transmit "thoughts poetic or otherwise," Pound could acknowledge no responsibility on the poet's part to his reader. The demands of an imbecilic public are no less opposed to the idea of a "pure" function for poetry than are the demands of any audience whatsoever whose language is the common one. Thus, Richard Aldington reminisced ironically that "the unforgivable sin of Imagist poetry" was that "people bought it."[48] For it seems that the imagist poet could have nothing to say to anyone; he had only this responsibility of maintaining a language in which something could be said. One cannot, of course, communicate with an audience unless one is concerned with its demands and expectations, but Pound's purpose seemed to free him from such concerns, for he considered poetry to precede any such purpose. It exists in order to ensure that the audience makes the right demands and has the right expectations because its language is healthy, so that those who may wish to use it to communicate might be able to do so.

Such a stance is not without irony, of course. John Gould Fletcher reminisced about modern poetry in terms that show us the outcome of such a view of the audience in practice: "In these ultramodern poets," he wrote, "thought has so far outrun verbal expression, that the authors concerned seem to be seeking for means of expressing some range of thought that is altogether so peculiar to themselves as to be inexpressible in any definite terms that we know. Poetry, to them, has become a means of communicating, to an increasingly dwindling audience, ranges of experience so far removed from the normal that only the practical and patient reader can make anything out of them. These poets have therefore been forced to defend themselves continually against the charge of obscurity."[49] The imagists, including Fletcher himself, chose to write for a "dwindling audience" by necessity, because of their attempts to oppose the communal nature of language and their desire to communicate experiences which were unique by definition. They were open to the charge of obscurity by virtue of the fact that if they had been understood by their contemporary audience, with its unhealthy language, they would have thought themselves to have failed.

One aspect of the romantic poet's relation to the audience, if we take the case of Coleridge, is that it became the reader's responsibility to make himself, so far as possible, into a poet, in order to understand the poem. Therefore, before he came to the poem, the reader's sensibilities had to be educated to come up to the poet's, in order for the communication to succeed. In earlier models of the poetic situation, it was the poet's assumption that a certain level of reader existed, a reader with whom the poet shared experiences. As Graham Hough has pointed out in his discussion of the background of the imagist revolt, the movement toward an elite sense of literature had been growing since the eighteenth century, because of the "cosmopolitanism" and "denationalization" of the audience.[50] Alexander Pope's ideal of "what oft was thought" and Samuel Johnson's notion of a "common reader" were no longer available in the nineteenth century, for a combination of such reasons, and perhaps such phenomena as the publication of Wordsworth's "Preface" can be understood to be a reaction to this growing uncertainty about who the audience was. To continue to be "a man speaking to men," the poet had to educate the audience to the new poetic, which included a new way of viewing experience. We can understand Pound's statement that poetry should be "a communication between intelligent men,"[51] in this same way, with the stress on "intelligent." The prescriptive impulse of the imagists can be better understood also if we view the various manifestos as written as much for the prospective audience of imagist poetry, to make it more "intelligent," as for the would-be imagist poet. To be able to read the poems, then, the audience was thought to require educating by some means other than by the poetry itself. The theory of imagism forbade the poet from attempting to communicate with an audience in a language not purified of convention. In response to this dilemma, the prose manifestos of the imagists took over one of the principal functions they intended for poetry: to alter the way people see reality by changing their attitude toward language. In a sense, then, the very existence of the manifestos is an admission of the failure of the poetry to accomplish this end, because no audience for the poetry could otherwise exist. One effect of the imagist program, then, was to put the burden of communication on the reader's shoulders. If the reader was not an imagist already, it seems that the poetry could do little to make him one. How then is the critical reader to approach the body of poems written by the imagists? Their distrust of the language inherited and expected by such a reader culminated in a distrust of rhetoric. We can begin to answer the question, perhaps, by turning now to the case against rhetoric, therefore, and to the concerns of the reader.

Chapter Two

RHETORICS

The process of invention is that of
gradually making solid the castles
in the air.
—T. E. Hulme

The Case Against Rhetoric

"Above all," Pound said of T. S. Eliot's poetry, "there is no rhetoric." He intended the remark as praise. But Eliot himself said, "Let us avoid the assumption that rhetoric is a vice of manner, and endeavor to find a rhetoric of substance also, which is right because it issues from what it has to express." Whether Eliot took Pound's remark as intended is therefore subject to some doubt, because he recognized the possibility of good and bad rhetorics, plural, whereas Pound condemned all rhetoric, singular. Whether or no, Pound illustrates a state of affairs that Eliot sought to correct. "We begin to suspect," said Eliot, that rhetoric "is merely a vague term of abuse for any style that is bad, that is so evidently bad or second-rate that we do not recognize the necessity for greater precision in the phrases we apply it to."[1] This lack of precision, and this self-evident assumption of the inferiority of poetry which is not imagistic, confronts us immediately when we ask the question: What did the imagists mean by *rhetoric*? I am trusting here that a measure of logomachy is tolerable if it leads to a clarification of the issues.

The instances in which the imagists actually used the word *rhetoric* are frequent, but, as one might expect, scattered throughout discussions of many other matters. There is no one place where any imagist produced a concerted attack on rhetoric. It was not, frankly, an issue for them. Their attitude toward rhetoric was more of an ubiquitous assumption, inherited from Yeats's generation, and the term offered itself as a ready-made pejorative to be applied in many contexts.

The most direct effect of the imagists' general speculations was the reform of certain linguistic practices in poetry, having to do with the economical and straightforward use of diction. In 1917 Harriet Monroe, who had published the earliest imagist manifestos in *Poetry* magazine, summed up this aspect of the movement by saying that "the truly modern poet rejects the so called 'poetic' shifts of language—the *deems*, *'neaths*, *forsooths*, etc., the inversions and high sounding rotundities, familiar to his predecessors: all the rhetorical excesses through which most Victorian poetry now seems 'over-appareled.'" The effect of these "rhetorical excesses" was assessed by Hulme: "It is a question of pitch; in romantic verse you move at a certain pitch of rhetoric which you know, man being what he is, to be a little high-falutin." The sort of rhetoric assumed to be found in such high-pitched earlier poetry was that which functioned to elevate plain statement, making it sound pompous, and the technical means of achieving this elevation were a lofty diction, inverted syntax, and the accumulation of unnecessary words. Fletcher shows how the term was taken for granted in a catalog of the abuses he cites in a review: "Tortured inversions, clever Elizabethan conceits, pedantic archaisms, over-strained rhetoric."[2]

Fletcher correctly credited Pound's special dislike for the poetry of Milton to all of these qualities. Pound saw in Milton the epitome of the rhetorical in this technical sense: "All this clause structure modelled on Latin rhetoric." Milton's name hardly ever crossed Pound's lips without the label "rhetoric" being applied to denigrate him, and all those who owed anything to him. "The younger generation," said Pound, has been "poisoned in the cradle by the abominable dogbiscuit of Milton's rhetoric." He asserted that Milton modeled himself on "rhetorical bustuous rumpus," as did the Pre-Raphaelites. He called Milton's style "a bombastic and rhetorical Elizabethan, coming from an attempt to write English with Latin syntax," and similarly assessed the Elizabethans in general, whose influence the present generation had not escaped. "After Villon," he said,

> and having begun before his time, we find this *fioritura*, and for centuries we find little else. Even in Marlowe and Shakespeare there is this embroidery of language, *this talk about the matter, rather than presentation.* I doubt if anyone ever acquired discrimination in studying "The Elizabethans." You have grace, richness of language, abundance, *but you have probably nothing that isn't replaceable by something else, no ornament that wouldn't have done just as well in some other connection, or for which some other figure of rhetoric couldn't have served.* . . . "Poetry" was considered to be (as it still is considered by a great number of drivelling imbeciles) synonymous with "*lofty and flowery language.*"[3]

"Rhetoric" could be used to name the qualities which had once distinguished "poetry." In insisting that "poetry should be at least as well written as prose," Pound and the imagists sought to eliminate the wordy circumlocutions which found their way so easily into poetry which sought to attain a "lofty pitch," but which, when judged by the prosaic standard of function, were unnecessary. F. S. Flint said that among the "devices whereby they persuaded approaching poetasters to attend their instructions" was to rewrite the poet's verses "before his eyes, using ten words to his fifty." *Rhetoric* was the term applied to those words and phrases which could be cut in this way, supposedly with no loss to the sense. Thus, in the technical respect, *rhetoric* meant ornament. It was used in this sense repeatedly by the imagists in their most generalized statements of policy, such as when Flint said, typically, "The function of *vers libre* was to strip poetry of rhetoric."[4]

As well as being a handy shorthand way of labeling all of the technical abuses which the imagists identified in others' poetry and tried to escape in their own, the term *rhetoric* also referred to the ends which technique is designed to serve. This is evident in Pound's statement about Shakespeare and Marlowe above, in which ornament is identified with "talk about the matter, rather than presentation," the latter being, as we have seen, the aim of the poet who is recording emotions in the manner of a scientist. For the imagists, rhetorical and nonrhetorical poetry, although identifiable by the presence or absence of features such as inversion, were ultimately distinguishable according to function. The absence of "rhetoric" in poetry was a sign of the presence of other qualities. As Richard Aldington put it, "The absence of the accepted rhetorical devices . . . force[s] both writer and reader to look for more essential qualities." Thus, the ornamental was not merely understood to have the function of decoration, but of obscuring the "essential." Remy de Gourmont had lamented how this affects the poet: "The ages of faith have heaped upon our minds such amassments of rhetoric . . . that now, when we seek natural explanations for lofty and beautiful things, we seem to commit a coarse triviality." Or worse, as Herbert Read was later to write of the poetry of Thomas Hardy: "It is not poetic—rather it is rhetorical, and like all rhetoric, a corruption of the poetic consciousness."[5] Just how the imagists themselves viewed rhetoric as a corruption of poetic consciousness will be our next concern.

Pound created a definition of rhetoric in the context of discussing the presence of images in earlier poets, and expressed a similar attitude: "Dante is a great poet by reason of this faculty [*i.e.* image making], and Milton is a wind-bag because of his lack of it. The 'image' is the furthest possible remove from rhetoric. *Rhetoric is the art of dressing up some unimportant matter so as to fool the audience for the time being.* So much for the general category. Even Aristotle distinguishes between rhetoric, 'which is persuasion,' and the analytic examination of the truth." Insofar as Pound appealed here to Aristotle's distinction between rhetoric and dialectic, this last statement is more or less accurate, but misleading. By suggesting that for Aristotle "the truth" provides the subject matter of art and only "unimportant matters" provide the subject matter of rhetoric, Pound misrepresented the parallel relationship which Aristotle saw between the arts of dialectic and rhetoric. Furthermore, he carried on the assumption that ornament can only obscure, since its presence indicates that the truth is not the subject. Yet he allowed for the use of ornament which does not obscure the truth, by telling the potential imagist poet to "use either no ornament, or good ornament."[6] This is a distinction, ironically, which corresponds exactly to Aristotle's, in his discussion of metaphor in the *Rhetoric*. Aristotle divided metaphor into two types: that which functions to increase perspicuity and that which functions merely for decoration.

If we look at Aristotle's discussion of metaphor in the *Rhetoric*, Book III, we actually find Pound's ideas prefigured. Aristotle clearly favored the use of metaphor when it functions to make style perspicuous, and such metaphors he styled "appropriate," meaning that they "observe due proportion," are not "far-fetched," and "give names to things that have none by deriving the metaphor from what is akin . . . so that, as soon as it is uttered, it is clearly seen to be akin." He objected to the use of metaphor when it produces what he called "frigidity," as when metaphors are chosen merely for their "strangeness." In giving examples of such metaphors, it is clear that not only did Aristotle consider that the inappropriate metaphor reduces perspicuity, but it also adds words unnecessarily:

> That is why the style of Alcidamas appears frigid; for he uses epithets not as a seasoning but as a regular dish, so crowded, so long, and so glaring are they. For instance, he does not say "sweat" but "damp sweat"; not "to the Isthmian games" but "to the solemn assembly of the Isthmian games"; not "laws" but "the laws, the rulers of states"; . . . Hence those who employ poetic language by their lack of taste make the style ridiculous and frigid, and such idle chatter produces obscurity; for when words are piled upon one who already knows, it destroys perspicuity by a cloud of verbiage.[7]

With updated examples, Pound's campaign against superfluous adjectives was a direct echo of Aristotle. Similarly, Pound discussed two functions of metaphor and postulated two types. He said, in a footnote to his edited text of Fenollosa's essay, "The poet . . . must . . . see to it that language does not petrify on his hands. He must prepare for new advances along the lines of true metaphor, that is interpretive metaphor, or image, as diametrically opposed to untrue, or ornamental, metaphor." We find the same distinction invoked in his essay on Guido Cavalcanti: "The difference between Guido and Petrarch is not a difference in degree, it is a difference in kind. . . . In Guido the 'figure,' the strong metaphoric or 'picturesque' expression is there with purpose to convey or to interpret a definite meaning. In Petrarch it is ornament, the prettiest ornament he could find, but not an irreplaceable ornament, or one that couldn't have been used just about as well somewhere else." The "irreplaceable ornament," presumably, is that sort of ornament which the imagist may use. Pound used the phrase, itself a contradiction in terms, as a synonym for the "interpretive metaphor," the image—which was ornamental, then, but only in some essential way. Pound liked to think of rhetorical figures as different in kind, as nonessential, replaceable ornament. Similarly, Amy Lowell defined the essential quality of the new poetry as "concentration . . . the discarding of all extraneous detail which tends to blur or diminish the vividness of the main theme. In architecture this has always been a cardinal principle—that all ornament should follow the structural line." Some criterion for "good ornament" similar to Aristotle's "appropriateness" was being sought by Pound and Lowell alike. Pound provided one also, when he wrote that "bad verbalism is rhetoric, or the use of *cliché* unconsciously, or a mere playing with phrases. But there is a good verbalism, distinct from lyricism or imagism, and in this LaForgue is the master. He writes not the popular language of any country but an international tongue common to the excessively cultivated, and to those more or less familiar with French literature of the first three-fourths of the nineteenth century."[8] "Good verbalism," although distinct here from the method of imagism, turns out to be that sort which is constructed to suit the audience by whom the poet wishes to be read, just as for Aristotle the particular audience must quickly be able to perceive the likeness of the metaphoric comparison for it to be successful. "Bad verbalism" can be distinguished by virtue of its redundancy for such an audience.

With all of this in mind, how can we justify Pound's use of the word *rhetoric* to signify "bad verbalism" only? Although the distinctions which Pound and Aristotle drew are parallel, the assignation of "rhetoric" to one or the other category is reversed. That is, for Aristotle, "rhetoric" consisted in the use of appropriate, nonornamental metaphors, whereas for Pound the same term denoted the use of inappropriate, ornamental metaphors. Aside from considerable historical slippage in the meaning of the term, some more fundamental distinction lies behind Pound's case against rhetoric, against the Aristotle who wrote an art of persuasion as opposed to the Aristotle who stood for "the analytic examination of the truth."

We can isolate this conflict by looking at the context in which Aristotle discussed metaphor in the *Rhetoric*. For him, rhetoric concerned both the discovery of what to say (the process of "invention") and the discovery of how it must be said (*e.g.* the processes of "arrangement" and "style"). Both kinds of discovery are necessary parts of that art which consists, not of persuasion itself, but of *discovering the available means* of persuasion in any given situation. When Aristotle turned to the subject of style as an available means, he said, "In regard to style, one of its chief merits may be defined as perspicuity," and for Aristotle perspicuity was the result of *concealing the artifice of the invention process* in order to render the thought more understandable and therefore more persuasive. "For that which is natural persuades," said Aristotle, "but the artificial does not." The art of style, therefore, was considered to be the art of rendering the artificial in such a way that it appears natural, and thus Aristotle said of inappropriate metaphors that "they exceed the dignity of the subject, and so the artifice can be seen." Again, he said, "if epithets are employed to excess, they reveal the art and make it evident that it is poetry." This attitude toward style persisted in the rhetorical tradition through Cicero's dictum: *ars est celare artem* (the art consists in concealing the art). The rhetor, that is, was assumed to face stylistic choices, all of which are artificial because all are among the discoverable available means, but more or less appropriate depending on their capacity to appear "natural." In order, thus, to know what means will bring about this end, the rhetor had to know the conventions of response which were shared by his audience, *i.e.* what means had worked in the past.

Thus, in the opening paragraph of his treatise, Aristotle stated the relationship between theory and practice which guided his inquiries. He first distinguished rhetoric as an "art" from the skill of persuasion, which is random or a knack acquired from practice. Then he said, "But since both these ways are possible, it is clear that matters can be reduced to a system, for it is possible to examine the reason why some attain their end by familiarity and others by chance; and such an examination all would at once admit to be the function of an art."[9] As a "system," or method, then, rhetoric is dependent on understanding the causes which lead to desired effects in the audience, and since these causes can be investigated, the *art* of rhetoric is practiced in relation to certain principles. It is rule-guided, because persuasion has causes, but not rule-governed, because efficacy is the standard. Although the principles of rhetoric may have had their origins in "natural" processes, when they are viewed as method they become artifice.

For Pound, the function of literature "is *not* the coercing or emotionally persuading, or bullying or suppressing people into the acceptance of any one set or any six sets of opinions as opposed to any other one set or half-dozen sets of opinions." Instead, he said, "its force will lie in its truth, its interpretive power. . . . I mean it will not try to seem forcible by rhetorical din." His argument with Aristotle, however, goes deeper than this distinction between persuasion and truth, because it implies that if the truth were stated, pure and simple, no rhetoric would be needed, that truth needs no means of persuasion. (This matter will concern us further in Chapter Five.) Pound was also fundamentally opposed to the relationship which Aristotle portrayed between the discovery of the materials of discourse and their application: between theory and practice. This is because, for Pound, no positive principles can guide the discovery of truth. Nothing comparable to the "artifice" in Aristotle's idea of invention exists for Pound. The Aristotelian notion of "art" as method contradicts the imagistic notion of poetry as accidental perception, which may thus be said to oppose the "rhetoric" of Aristotle at its most fundamental point. Whereas "naturalness" is an effect created by conscious effort in Aristotle's conception of style, for Pound nature and artifice are mutually exclusive, and artifice is not art because "art exists as the trees exist." To search for the "exact word," which is the image, one must possess the experiential paradigm as a given. The notion of an *exact* word, central to imagist theory, means that there is only one image for each unique experience, making the process "natural" from beginning to end. One does not look to the audience for a clue to this image, as one does by pursuing topical invention in Aristotle. Any thought to his audience leads the poet astray. He should look instead to his experience, which alone determines the poet's choices.

If such is the case, however, the image cannot be said to be "chosen." Pound made this crucial distinction: "In verse," he said, "something has come upon the intelligence. In . . . prose the intelligence has found a subject for its observations. *The poetic fact pre-exists.*"[10] How can a poetic fact *pre-exist*? What is a poetic *fact*? In this statement of Pound's lies the central concept of his anti-rhetorical stance, the idea that poetry expresses truths which have eternal existence apart from and prior to their expression, and the poet writes falsely, therefore, if he imposes any willful choice upon their selection. In effect, this concept of the poetic process denies the possibility of speaking of poetic "invention." The poet must have the intelligence to seize an opportunity, for Pound, but unless this "something" occurs, in the form of a uniquely poetic experience, intelligence alone is useless. At least, it is useful only to produce prose in which one has something to say and searches for the best way to say it. It almost seems that the imagist, finally, had nothing of his own to say. Needless to say, this view exactly corresponds to Hulme's metaphysical forms of perception. To see into "the thing itself," which also "pre-exists," is a matter of receiving intuitive glimpses of reality, accidental glimpses which no conscious effort is able to bring about. Conscious effort, rather, destroys this intuition of the truth, and so rhetoric becomes "the art of dressing up some unimportant matter so as to fool the audience." Only by escaping rhetoric can the poet be gifted with the ability to perceive and record the "poetic fact."

The ontology of imagism depended on this psychical ability of the poet.[11] As we have seen, on the testimony of Aldington and Gourmont, when a poet produces rhetoric it is a sign that he is not seeing, not thinking, in the right way. Pound made the same distinction along historical lines when he wrote, "The Renaissance sought a realism and attained it. It rose in a search for precision and declined through rhetoric and rhetorical thinking, through a habit of defining always 'in terms of something else.'"[12] The rhetorical artifacts in the poem could not be disassociated from the way of thinking which brought them forth. To seek "a realism" was a motive which produced the precision of utterance which imagism demanded, but to think rhetorically produced the sorts of verbal rhetoric to which the imagists objected, figures which distorted the poet's vision. These figures resulted from habits of seeing a thing in terms of something else: Hulme's definition of the relational "analytic" conventions which veil perception.

In 1902, Remy de Gourmont described the writing of the Port Royalists in terms which were naturally attractive to his imagist followers: "Exempt from art to an inconceivable degree, Port Royal cultivated," he said, "wretched rhetorical flowers in a sorry garden. It is disloyal to confuse art with rhetoric. . . . Rhetoric is the putting into practice processes of the art of writing previously dissected by a clever man. . . . Art is the spontaneous and ingenious exercise of natural talent." By opposing art to rhetoric in this way, Gourmont also opposed it to style, if style requires the application of techniques acquired from literary sources. The artist's style, as opposed to the rhetorician's, will follow no laws; only by being unique can it "incorporate the writer's sensibility," as Gourmont said. From the psychological perspective of the imagists' generation, Richard Aldington put it this way: "Sincerity," he said, "is an examination of self to discover whether one really has anything worth saying, or, in other words, whether one has personality. The external mark of personality is style. By style I do not mean that 'correctness' of schoolmasters, and professors, which is a dead rhetoric." Thus, for Pound, technique is "the test of a man's sincerity,"[13] as if by the absence of rhetorical devices one could know that a poet was telling the truth. The sparseness of the imagist style, then, can be accounted for, in part, because technique was considered to consist in not adding anything to the "poetic fact" that would distort it. Style, for the imagists, was a negative, almost a passive, concept. The fact that the imagists shared *a* style, however, which they could acquire and apply, would tend to

compromise the radical split between rhetoric and art, if Gour-
mont's criteria prevailed.

Rhetoric, then, denoted whatever had been done before, or
convention in the full sense in which Hulme used the word, and
Pound when he said that "the function of art is to free the intellect
from the tyranny of . . . conventions." Hulme's notion of "con-
ventional thinking" coincides with Pound's "rhetorical thinking,"
a state of mind which is based on imitation or habit and which al-
lows only for those perceptions which can be made to fit the con-
ventional patterns. Pound called these patterns by Gourmont's
term, "the shells of thought," ideas whose validity is somehow
questioned because they have an abstractable similarity to other
ideas. Pound, we recall, regarded poetry as a way to restore "va-
lidity" to language, and therefore to allow the mind to function
properly. Hulme expressed a similar idea by comparing the actions
of the mind to drawing with an architect's curve.[14] Using such a
device, said Hulme, the architect can produce only those curves
which are found along its edge, and he is prevented, by the instru-
ment itself, from rendering any object which has curves unique to
itself. All his drawings become, therefore, approximations. And
so it is with thought which confines itself to patterns such as logic.
Rhetoric, then, was considered as a sort of template, a habitual
way of using language to express commonplace ideas, and, as a
limited set of choices, it similarly prevents the expression of "the
exact curve of the thing," to use Hulme's phrase. Rhetoric, there-
fore, was thought to serve only the expression of some worn-out
doctrine. But to express the exact word which is unique to a par-
ticular experience, rhetoric would not serve. Like the architect,
the rhetorician produces approximations of what he desires to say.
Rhetorical thinking, as "defining always in terms of something
else," leads to the approximate perception of comparative relation-
ships between emotion and nature, rather than the exact percep-
tion of their identity.

The metaphor, wrote Fenollosa, is an "identity of structure."
He said, as we have already seen, that "the transferences of force
from agent to object, which constitute natural phenomena, oc-
cupy time. Therefore, a reproduction of these in imagination re-

quires the same temporal order." To this passage in the essay, Pound appended this puzzling footnote: "Style, that is to say, limpidity, as opposed to rhetoric." The note comes clear when we realize that *rhetoric* is used here in the sense that we have just seen. According to Fenollosa, language itself operates according to nature's laws: agent-act-object, subject-verb-object. Should some inversion of rhetoric place the verb before the subject, it is more than syntax which has been disrupted, it is the order of nature itself. To have "limpidity," *i.e.* such transparency of language that the words are the things they represent ("the application of word to thing"), one cannot have rhetoric. Rhetoric, after all, is thinking like language, and language has lost its contact with nature. "Thinking," said Fenollosa, "is *thinging*, to follow the buds of fact as they open and see thought folded away within thought like so many petals."[15]

Style, then, for the imagists, is not governed by the laws of language, but by the laws of nature, "the inevitable laws of nature," as Pound called them. Again, it was Gourmont who provided the model for this view, when, in discussing "style without rhetoric," he advocated that "there is only one style: an involuntary style, whether rich or poor, imaged or naked. . . . It suffices to avoid all rhetoric, to use no word when one is not sure of its meaning—that is, its symbolic connection with reality—to speak only of what one has seen, heard, felt." That the process of recording the terms of reality is "involuntary" meant that the poet exercised no choice, just as for Hulme the perception of the image was an "unlooked-for resemblance." Avoiding all rhetoric meant, quite simply, relinquishing that aspect of the poetic act which is willful. Amy Lowell praised the poetry of John Gould Fletcher by saying that its "observation is very minute and exact. This is the more remarkable when we think how often he must have to subdue his imagination to let reality print itself upon him with the force which it does."[16] To subdue the imagination seems to have been the means of discovering a truer reality, and rhetoric, for the imagists, represented the artist's attempt to control a process of discovery as opposed to this submission to nature. The net effect, in imagism, of the attempt to get rid of rhetoric, then, even by their own definition of the term, was to substitute for the will a sense of poetic invention bereft of control and reduced to impulse.[17]

Control, as I have used it here, should not be confused with labor. The imagists' advocacy of technique certainly involved them in a laborious and well-documented process of revision. To say that imagism's antipathy toward rhetoric represented a relinquishing of control over poetic invention, therefore, requires a sense of the difference between technique as an aspect of invention and technique as a sort of afterthought. Technique seems to have been a matter of recapturing an undistorted view of reality which was itself only possible by escaping technique. The stance is indeed paradoxical. In an attempt to foreclose just such an analysis of imagism as I have given here, Hugh Kenner, in *The Poetry of Ezra Pound*, wrote that "Pound's strictures on rhetoric" should not "be confused with the romantic-Ockhamist opinion of Croce (the most familiar modern anti-rhetorician) that once the aesthetic intuition is formulated no expanding, re-shaping, or rehandling is valid. It would be puzzling if Pound, the technician *par excellence*, could be identified with an opposition to rhetorical artifice that was really a disguise for the romantic opposition to the artist's employment of conscious procedures." Kenner's view of the problem, however, should be seen in the light of Pound's own statements on the relationship between impulse and technique. He wrote in 1913, for instance, that "there's no use in a strong impulse if it is nearly all lost in bungling transmission and technique. This obnoxious word that I'm always brandishing about means nothing but a transmission of the impulse intact."[18]

Pound was indeed a master of technique, but he saw it as a potential obstacle as much as a resource. Since technique is enigmatically equated with the "transmission of the impulse intact," it seems that it consisted in avoiding such ways of writing that would obscure the impulse. It seems that how a thing is said is entirely determined by the nature of the impulse itself, and the lack of control that applies to the discovery of what to say manifests itself in technique as a predetermined process. The imagist ideal of employing technique to find the "exact word,"—almost to carve this preexisting word out of a ponderous mass of words —suggests that conscious control serves the intuition in a frankly deterministic manner. Imagist technique, as Aldington said, was a matter of discovering whether one has anything to say. "All poetic language," according to Pound, "is the language of exploration."[19] If the object of this exploration is something true about the self, then it seems that the ideal of poetic language sought by the imagists—despite the labor involved in excising old poetic habits—can indeed be equated with the "romantic opposition to the artist's employment of conscious procedures." Conscious procedures extended to getting the rhetoric out of the way so that the impulse could be transmitted "intact," in whatever form this impulse demanded. If no conventional habits were part of the poet's mental processes, then technique would not be necessary—and this convention-free state of mind was imagism's aim.

Pound followed his remark on technique as the transmission of the impulse by saying, "It means you not only get a thing off your own chest, but you get it into some one else's." Insofar as such a statement entails a theory of communication, it is necessary to turn once again to the reader, and to the assumptions about intention which operate when one confronts a poem with the idea of understanding it. Pound's statement makes it plain that the reader was never entirely out of the picture in imagist poetics, and to see why we must consider whether the antirhetorical ideals of imagism necessarily give way to other concerns.

Rhetoric and Reading

The act of purposeful reading implies the act of purposeful writing. It consists in an effort to understand what a poem means, implying that it means something by design. Granting the validity of arguments for an "intentional fallacy," we might say that this activity consists of the formulation, by way of the text, of *an* intention which is sufficient to account for everything that is actually done in the text. The perspective of the reader, which I introduced at the beginning, with its axiom about the relation of means and ends, requires the formulation of intention as the discoverable end

which accounts for the means used in a text. That is, in respond-
ing to a work the reader is aware of being moved by its strategies
and seeks to understand the experience of those strategies by ask-
ing: "To what end am I being put through this?" The intentional
fallacy teaches that we must be wary of identifying our answer to
this question as "intention" in the sense of the real motive of the
biographical poet, but a sense of an assumed intention, and the ne-
cessity of discovering it, is nevertheless a component of the act of
reading.[20] Understanding is the name we apply to the state in
which we feel assured that we have discovered that end which ren-
ders the means of the work both necessary and sufficient. We are
able to answer the question, "Why *this* poem, *this* way?" The
ways of a poem include what its statements signify as well as how
they manage to evoke responses that have no semantic equivalent.
That is, words have the power to *do* as well as to *say*, and poetry
must be considered to be a form of discourse in which the doing is
as important as the saying. It is no less true, however, that what a
poem *means to do* is a discoverable and testable formulation. Even
though we may never be assured, of course, that we have met the
author on the level of his purpose, we could not begin to attempt
the discovery of a poem's ontology without the assumption that
an intention, to say or do something, exists.

As the classical scholar H. D. F. Kitto reminds us, such an act
of purposeful reading depends on yet another assumption, rarely
stated but necessary if we are to avoid making every act of reading
into an act of self-discovery only. That is the assumption that the
poet has not only chosen to do something to us, but that he was in
control of the process of doing it. Without the assumption of con-
trol we run the risk of misinterpretation whenever our "unchal-
lenged and unsuspected presuppositions" interfere with what the
text actually says. "If there is a conflict between one of these and
the text," Kitto says, ironically, "it is the text that must give way.
We read the words, but they do not bite into our minds; the temp-
tation to make them accord with what we *know* the [author] must
have meant is irresistible."[21] We have no more means of knowing
that an author was in fact in control than we have of knowing that
we have in fact understood his intention, but without either *as-*

sumption our reading becomes a matter of gratifying our desires rather than fulfilling an act of communication. To assume that the author has done what he has done by choice, even though our conclusions of what he has done must remain open to reconsideration, is to read as if we wanted to understand.

The problem of how to understand an imagist poem, then, comes down to the question of whether or not we concede the theoretical demand that the poet must relinquish control over the poetic act, as we have just seen the rejection of rhetoric to entail. If rhetoric, to the imagists, meant purposeful control over the choices made by the writer, then we must assume that the poem has a rhetoric in order to read it. Insofar as we allow our reading to be guided by the imagists' desire to escape the will, we admit that the poetry is not subject to the sort of reading experience I have just described, *i.e.* not subject to interpretation. Or else we allow our interpretation to be guided by no principle of necessity.

One consequence of the imagists' theoretical desire to write with no rhetoric, with no conscious design to hinder the "rendering of the impulse," therefore, would be a sort of wishful interpretation which permits the free associations of the reader to constitute a valid part of a poem's meaning. One does not have to search far for an apparent example of criticism of this sort. Ezra Pound's famous imagistic couplet, "In a Station of the Metro,"

> The apparition of these faces in a crowd:
> Petals on a wet, black bough.

for example, is given the following reading by Hugh Kenner in *The Pound Era*:

This is not any crowd, moreover, but a crowd seen underground, as Odysseus and Orpheus and Koré saw crowds in Hades. And carrying forward the suggestion of wraiths, the word "apparition" detaches these faces from all the crowded faces, and presides over the image that conveys the quality of their separation:

> Petals on a wet, black bough.

Flowers, underground; flowers out of the sun; flowers seen as if against a natural gleam, the bough's wetness gleaming on its darkness, in this place where wheels turn and nothing grows. The mind is touched, it may be, with a memory of Persephone, as we read of her in the 106th Canto,

> Dis' bride, Queen over Phlegethon,
> girls faint as mist about her.

—the faces of these girls likewise "apparitions."

Kenner's conclusions, that the scene is associated with Hades, that the faces are detached from the crowd, that the poem may touch the mind with "a memory of Persephone," are clearly occasioned by the poem, but they cannot be said to be controlled by it. Although Kenner admits that the association with Persephone "may be," he later credits the poem with "drawing on" this memory, and adds even more associations to the list: "So this tiny poem," he writes, "drawing on Gauguin and on Japan, on ghosts and on Persephone, on the Underworld and on the Underground, the Metro of Mallarmé's capital and a phrase that names a station of the Metro as it might a station of the Cross, concentrates far more than it need ever specify." [22]

Now, a poem need not specify all of the meaning which it concentrates, but certainly there must be an internal limit on the meanings which it permits, based on what is within control, even if that limit is as vague as a plausible relevance. In bringing into play such unrelated associations as the Stations of the Cross, Mallarmé, Persephone, Gauguin, and Koré, Kenner seems to have exceeded this limit. Whatever unifies these associations, it is not anything in the poem, which does not need them to be understood. The reductio of Kenner's method, as exemplified here, is that a poem can mean anything that it happens to remind the reader of, with no obvious controls governing the reader's choices, with the result that such criticism tells us less of the poet's meaning than of the critic's. It is to read without the assumption of intention—the assumption which makes reading an act of communication rather than an act of self-discovery. Assuming that a poet has controlled his choice of what goes into a poem, in order to control the reader's response, is what makes reading the potential discovery of what the poet has been able to do. Insofar as Kenner is attempting to make a method of reading out of imagist theory, he is forced to read as if the poet had no purpose, even, in arranging words into sentences, and so he presumes that the reader is free to rearrange them. And why not, if, as he says, "syntax is a one-way street, its principals and subordinates guiding us with sometimes misleading ease through a sentence or a poem. . . . But lay out, instead, the elements all on one plane, each sharp, each bright, each of comparable importance; disregard their syntactic liaisons; make a selection, and arrange them anew, as the cubists arranged visual elements so that one cannot say what is theme, what is detail."[23] To the degree that one accepts the imagists' claims to have desired not to guide the reader through a process, one is constrained to view syntax in this manner. The cubists are presumed by Kenner to have controlled their paintings in order to create this experience in the viewer because the paintings are unsyntactical. But he does not consider the same control to apply to the syntactical arrangements of the imagists. The inconsistency results from trying to read the poems to fit the theory, in spite of how they are written.

I do not mean to suggest that Kenner willfully ignores the poem in favor of a merely private set of associations. He is, of course, seeking understanding of the poem and the associations which he cites might be said to fall within what E. D. Hirsch, Jr., after Husserl, has called the "horizon" of intention. It is a question, as always, of where this horizon is said to end. Can it take in, for instance, an association, like Kenner's "underground," of which there is no evidence that the author was consciously aware but which nevertheless can be seen as a potential means of communicating something? Yes, of course, depending on the plausibility of the critic's explanations of *how* the association functions in relation to the other parts of the poem. But can it take in, for instance, associations from another poem composed significantly later, as Kenner would have the "Metro" poem "draw on" Persephone from *Canto 106*? I think not, because there is no explanation of how it can be said to function as one of the poem's *means*. If the "horizon" of intention could take in such an association, then the term *intention* is being used to encompass both the "meaning" of the poem and its "significance," to cite a distinction also proposed by Hirsch. These two concepts, as Hirsch presents them, correspond to the kinds of responses I have called "controlled" and "occasioned," and they similarly refer to the metaphysical question of the mind's ability to perceive meaning as stable from one context to another. Meaning, then, is a more elemental concept than significance, which refers to "textual meaning as related to some context, indeed any context, beyond itself." While one cannot pretend to be able to know a poem as a thing itself, without a context, and this will always be cited as a reason for preferring significance over meaning, yet it should be said that if the distinction is accepted a poem must have meaning before it can be said to have significance, which is defined as its meaning perceived in some relation to something else. My argument with Kenner, then, over his interpretation of Pound's couplet, is not that he desires to relate it to other contexts of meaning, but that he seems to do so without first answering the question of meaning as a relationship of means to ends. And my point is that if meaning, as Hirsch says, "cannot exceed the conventional semantic *possibilities* of the symbols used,"[24] then the task of discovering meaning involves the question of what conventions the poem employs and what responses these conventions are capable of controlling. Since imagism seeks to deny both the use of convention and the desirability of control, as I have said, it leaves the imagist reader with no recourse but to attempt to discover significance without a core of meaning. And without this core, there is nothing to ratify whether a significance is plausible.

We can reconstruct a perspective which renders the imagist poem understandable by reinvesting the poet with the control of which the theory divests him. The imagists, despite their most radical stances, invite us to do so by their inconsistencies. Despite the fact that rhetoric was considered to be the domination of the will over the style that is given by nature, for instance, we also find Pound defining style as "the absolute subjugation of the details of a given work to the dominant will; to the central urge or impulse." In saying this, Pound admitted that the details of the poem are made consistent with some end, and that style can be understood, by the reader, through the discovery of that "dominant will" which accounts for those details. "All styles," said

Hulme, "are only means of subduing the reader."[25] Such statements suggest that the stances of the imagists against the construction of "rhetorical artifice" can be reevaluated in light of other considerations.

We have already seen, for instance, that although the imagists sought to escape the idea that poetry was a "vehicle" for communicating ideas, they merely substituted for the concept "communication" the new term "direct communication." Whatever form such communication was meant to have, this much is implied by the term: The imagists, while denying the reader's role in poetic invention, do wish to assert some control over what happens to their readers, on the assumption that a certain sort of poetic experience is desirable. If so, then it seems that they must also accept some part of the "burden of communication," after all. In other words, they must have assumed some of the responsibility for seeing that the reader's experience was of the sort they desired. Does the acceptance of this burden also commit the imagists to using traditional literary conventions, no matter how such an idea might conflict with their metaphysics?

To answer this question we must turn again, briefly, to the nature of the imagists' attitude toward the audience, and the nature of the conventions of literary response which writer and reader must share in order for communication, in any form, to come about. As I have already said, the manifestos of imagism, the prose statements of poetic intention, served the purpose of educating an audience to the values and techniques of the new poetry. In their authors' view, the existing audience was corrupt, making it necessary to create an audience based on a certain ideal reader. This new audience was not an imaginary hypothesization, however. The revolutionary thrust of the imagists' manifestos constitutes a sign of their confidence that this new audience could be made from the existing one. If the corruption of the existing audience was viewed as the result of "conventional thinking," then the task of creating the new audience required the abolition of such thinking, the destruction, in other words, of stereotyped ways of responding to poems. The new poetry, in 1912, did not seem to be poetry at all to those conservative readers whose expectation of poetry required that it be metered, for instance, and the imagists spent considerable energy arguing against this prejudice. To dissolve such expectations was prerequisite to making an audience capable of responding to imagist poetry as the imagists intended. This could also be seen as the basis for their attacks on the "rhetorical" devices of the Victorians. But there was a constructive side to the propaganda as well, of course. The imagists sought to replace the old habits of the contemporary reader with new ways of responding to poems which were consistent with the new ways the poets were being encouraged, at the same time, to write them. Our problem here is to say whether these new ways of responding were not necessarily conventional in the same sense as the discarded habits, and whether the patterns of response demanded by imagist poems are not, in certain ways, identical to those demanded by any sort of poem, including the sort the imagists sought to abolish.

Indeed, we face the question of whether conventional patterns of response can be abandoned at all once they are established. That is, although it is easy to see how an audience can be educated to accept new ways of responding to poetry, it is difficult to conceive of the possibility of preventing them from responding to certain structures as they always had. No poetic revolt, it seems, is able to overturn every aspect of its rejected predecessor. Something of the old must remain. The imagists may have succeeded in creating an audience which could accept the new, or the absence of certain expected conventions, but they could hardly succeed in suppressing conventional responses to patterns which are as much a part of their poetry as a part of Victorian poetry. To argue for the elimination of conventional responses is not enough, perhaps, unless all those patterns which are capable of being responded to conventionally are also avoided, and this is something which was not done in imagist poems (as the remaining chapters attempt to show). If the poets used conventional patterns, they must have expected their readers to respond in conventional ways. The irony of revolt, perhaps, is that it can never be complete and still be understood.[26]

Hulme proposed the following explanation for the mechanics

of the image. "The main function of analogy," he said, "is to enable one to dwell and linger upon a point of excitement. To achieve the impossible and convert a point into a line. This can only be done by having ready-made lines in our heads, and so getting at the result by analogy." To convert a point into a line is Hulme's metaphor for the sort of continuously present "instant" which the imagists desired the reader to experience. Analogy provided the means for achieving this result for another reason than its capacity to stimulate the intuition, according to Hulme in this passage. Analogy is an appeal to a "ready-made" pattern, a convention. In an admission such as this, and in the very distinction which the imagists created between communication and direct communication, lies an awareness of a commonplace in modern criticism, at least since Saussure. That is the idea that, as Jonathan Culler has recently summarized it, "the communicative intention presupposes listeners who know the language." Language, here, means *langue*, the conventional operations of the system of language which all who understand a given utterance must know, exclusive of the utterance itself, *parole*. Recent critics have adopted Chomsky's terms to refer to the same distinction: competence and performance. The concept of linguistic competence has been used to explain "literary competence," or the knowledge of a system of literary meaning which makes the work communicable. "To intend a meaning," says Culler, "is to postulate reactions of an imagined reader who has assimilated the relevant conventions."[27]

It was precisely this fact about communication that the imagists desired to overcome, of course, since they blamed the limitations which the existence of conventions imposes on the mind for the inability of poetry to communicate certain kinds of meaning. That they wished to educate the reader to recognize new sorts of meanings—to make real readers in the image of their imagined readers—means, however, that they must have sought to create a new sort of literary competence, to substitute a new ideal basis of response which would allow the competent reader to grasp these new meanings. The central naïveté of imagism, perhaps, was that while tacitly recognizing the principle of conventional competence, they sought to abolish it. That is, in pursuit of the Bergsonian ideal of intuitive "direct" communication, Hulme, and Pound in his definition of the image, wished to create an ideal audience of convention-free readers, free of time and space limitations, readers whose response to the text of a poem would imitate the poet's response to the emotional meaning of "things." But the formulation of the text toward this end required the creation of some pattern in which the reader might be competent, either Hulme's "analogy," or Pound's "equation." Pound said, "By 'image' I mean . . . an equation; not an equation of mathematics, not something about *a*, *b*, and *c*, having to do with form, but about *sea*, *cliffs*, *night*, having something to do with mood."[28] Understanding the nature of this equation, presumably, is what allows the reader to respond to it properly, and for this reason such an equation can only be called a convention in the sense to which the imagists objected: it is constructed to appeal to a predisposition of the reader to respond in one way and not another. The reader's competence in the formula is what makes the communication, direct or indirect, possible.

So, despite the metaphysical quandary that such a statement put him in, Hulme called, in his notes, for "a new convention, to turn ourselves loose in." Literature, he said, is "a method of sudden arrangement of commonplaces. The *suddenness* makes us forget the commonplace."[29] These are moments in imagist theory when it is admitted that it is sufficient to make the reader think that what is really a convention is not a convention. If the reader cannot actually be brought to see the thing in its thing-ness, we might conclude, it might satisfy the imagist poet to convince the reader that he does. Such a possibility, however, based on such statements, destroys the distinction that I made earlier between Aristotle and Pound. It suggests that the image, from the reader's point of view, could not be trusted to do exactly what it was intended to do (*i.e.* communicate nature directly) and could only persuade us through artifice of an illusion of naturalness. Imagism called for the creation of conventions that were capable of persuading the reader that an unconventional glimpse into reality could be had.

So long as the imagists desired to communicate, directly, as they said, despite the ideal that the artist must remain indifferent to the conventional demands of the reader, they were necessarily concerned with effects. If the poem was not able to render the effect of the reality exactly as perceived, even though the poet was assured that he had found the "exact word" to "present" that reality accurately, the imagists would not consider a poem to succeed. What they evolved, then, were conventions, of necessity, for only by means of an assumption of some effect on the reader's part can an intended effect be in any way controlled. The antirhetorical commitment to breaking down and avoiding conventions transposes, therefore, into a rhetorical commitment to using conventions in order to control the reader's expectations and responses. We may not concede the poets' claims to have relinquished control over the selection and disposition of words based on the reader's, as opposed to nature's, necessities. The ideal reader of imagism was certainly not to be identified with the contemporary post-Victorian public, but neither was this ideal reader therefore a purely intuitive spirit whose responses were unguided by conventions, who brought to the poem no predisposition to respond in a certain way.

From this follows the possibility of identifying a "rhetoric of imagism," to be illustrated and discussed in the chapters that follow. This concept does not depend on the conclusion that the imagists failed in overturning the rhetorical techniques they scorned. It is to assert, however, that they left in the wake of their reforms a different body of rhetorical techniques, which operate according to the same principles as the old ones. This conclusion would, of course, turn Pound's complaint against Yeats back on himself, as he stated it in *Make It New*: "I remember Yeats: 'I have spent the whole of my life trying to get rid of rhetoric. . . . I have got rid of one kind of rhetoric and have merely set up another.'"[30] But it does not carry with it the same implication of failure. Nor does such a conception invalidate many of the arguments which the imagists made about the discarded techniques, and does not, therefore, put their technical reforms into question. It does, however, alter our view of how imagist poetry functions. It allows us to consider a way of reading imagist poetry which imagist theory, insofar as it is grounded on the premise that rhetoric is anathema to poetry, does not permit.

Those who have pointed to the discontinuity between the theory and the practice of the imagists have generally regarded the poetry as flawed because it did not measure up to the demands placed upon it by the theory. It might be argued, therefore, that so little consistent imagist poetry was written because the practitioners (not all of whom were theorists) did not understand the major aesthetic impulses of the movement. The point of view offered here allows for precisely the opposite conclusion. The poetry may be read as a consistent body of work, held together by discoverable principles. It is the theory, however, which has failed. If its principles are not the same as those found to constitute the functional coherence of the poetry, it is due to the impossibility of those principles. The fact that the theoretical demands are not heeded by the poets may be viewed as evidence of this impossibility, rather than as evidence of their failure to be pure imagists. Further, such a perspective provides good cause to take the poetry seriously, as poetry, rather than as applied theory, without the screen of prejudices that imagist assumptions usually create between the poetry and its critical audience. Imagist poetry does have means whereby it succeeds in communicating, but only at the expense of its most precious ideals. The ideals evolved from metaphysical speculations about what poetry, in the pure abstract, ought to be, but they failed the poets in the act of attempting to use the available means of language to make poems.

Chapter Three

TEXTURES

. . . the emotion of the thing.
—Ezra Pound

Hulme's Test

The subject is function. In what ways does the image work strategically to produce a certain effect in the reader? For the imagists, understanding images was the culmination of a simple chain of events: An "object," said T. E. Hulme, "must cause the emotion before [the] poem can be written." What the poet writes, the image, according to John Gould Fletcher, "is an analogy drawn between something external in nature and the feeling that arises within the observer." The final step, in the words of Ford Madox Ford, results because the poem "consists in so rendering concrete objects that the emotions produced by the objects shall arise in the reader."[1] The reader's experience reciprocates the poet's. The emotion caused in the poet by the object is the same emotion caused in the reader by the image of the same object.

The process as conceived by the imagists is thus made to work by the faithfulness with which the poet renders the perceived object. The poet was therefore required to attend to this faithfulness. "A man cannot write," said Hulme, "without seeing at the same time a visual signification before his eyes. It is this image which precedes the writing and makes it firm." Hence, "each *word* must be an image *seen*." Since the process of communication through such images is assumed to be directly reciprocal, the same criteria could become a test of poetry, to be applied by the reader: "Did the poet," Hulme asked, "have an actually realised visual object before him in which he delighted?"[2]

Such a conception of the poetic process was not the exclusive property of imagism, of course. In fact, it is quite commonplace. Somewhat before the imagist movement, the critic G. H. Lewes wrote that "an artist produces an effect in virtue of the distinctness with which he sees the object he represents." Shortly after imagism, J. G. Jennings wrote, similarly, that "in reading poetry one of the first necessities is to visualise, to see clearly every picture as it is presented by the poet. Without visualising the poet's words the reader in no sense has before him what the poet had at the time of writing. Nor can he in any full sense share his emotion."[3] Despite frequent warnings by subsequent critics against neglecting the conceptual element of imagery,[4] the mark of the persistence in our time of this imagist concept is a continued emphasis on visualization as a sense perception shared by the poet and the reader, and on the direct communication of emotion that is assumed to result from the accurate recording of the object of that perception. Such a statement as this by Laurence Perrine, for instance, in a popular textbook, would not strike the present-day reader as untypical: "The poet seeking to express his experience of a spring day must . . . provide a selection of the impressions he has. . . . Without doing so he will probably fail to evoke the emotions that accompanied his sensations. His language, therefore, must be more sensuous than ordinary language. It must be more full of imagery."[5] In such statements, however well qualified and even if not expressed prescriptively, Hulme's critical test lives on.

It is the question of the efficacy of this test that concerns us. In looking for a way to read imagist poems, we might ask whether this test can be applied, and whether the causal relation between object, image, and emotion assumed by the imagists actually accounts for our understanding of imagist poems. Before directly answering this question, I wish to discuss the effects created in typical imagist poems, and then to return to the question of the function of the image in light of these effects. Here are six short imagist poems:

New Love
Richard Aldington

She has new leaves
After her dead flowers,
Like the little almond-tree
Which the frost hurt.

The Skaters
John Gould Fletcher

Black swallows swooping or gliding
In a flurry of entangled loops and curves;
The skaters skim over the frozen river.
And the grinding click of their skates
    as they impinge upon the surface,
Is like the brushing together of thin
    wing-tips of silver.

Oread
H. D.

Whirl up, sea—
whirl your pointed pines,
splash your great pines
on our rocks
hurl your green over us
cover us with your pools of fir.

Liu Ch'e
Ezra Pound

The rustling of the silk is discontinued,
Dust drifts over the court-yard,
There is no sound of foot-fall, and the leaves
Scurry into heaps and lie still,
And she the rejoicer of the heart is beneath them:
A wet leaf that clings to the threshold.

The Sea Shell
Allen Upward

To the passionate lover, whose sighs come back to him
    on every breeze, all the world is like a murmuring
    sea-shell.

The Fisherman's Wife
Amy Lowell
When I am alone,
The wind in the pine trees
Is like the shuffling of waves
Upon the wooden sides of a boat.

I will discuss these poems individually in the next section of this chapter. For now, however, I wish only to observe that whatever differences they might exhibit, they share as a common denominator the convention of comparison, whether simple or complex, explicit or implicit. If there is a single paradigm according to which each of these poems functions, it is the underlying structure: x is like y. Not all of the poems reproduce this structure, to be sure, but they all seem to depend on it, nevertheless, as a conventional basis against which deviations are meaningful. A brief word about this convention is in order: Comparison functions *minimally* by requiring the reader to ascribe attributes to categories. For example, if I draw

   is like

the creation of this formula does not commit the perceiver to imagine some figure which incorporates both shapes. The existence of the second shape, rather, makes the perceiver return to the first, to see there attributes which might have otherwise been overlooked but which were there all along. We are forced to see the triangle, that is, as something sharing qualities with the other shape. (To "see" means to "understand" in this case; even this graphic comparison is apprehended cognitively.) We might conclude that this simile functions to draw our attention to the fact that the triangle is drawn in black ink, that it is composed of unbroken lines, or that it is asymmetrical. There is no new shape which the two shapes equal; there is only the first shape "seen" in terms in which we would ordinarily not have seen it. On the simplest level, then, the comparison "x is like y" must be said to be about *x*. "My love is like a red, red rose" does not tell us anything about roses. It brings certain qualities of "my love," shared by red roses, into prominence. Although we are certainly able to visualize the roses, it is not on this ability, specifically, that the comparison depends. If it were, then this comparison must be said to function in some other way than, say, W. H. Auden's "law like love," which makes similar cognitive demands but which is hardly able to be pictured. Without visualization, then, comparison is possible. Without attributing the qualities of one category to another, it is not.

Such a simple principle becomes important in the discussion of imagism when we consider that, theoretically, the image was intended, according to Hulme, to be "the *simultaneous* presentation to the mind of two different images," which "form what one might call a *visual chord*. They unite to suggest an image which is *different to both*."[6] Thus, to return to Pound's imagistic couplet, "In a Station of the Metro," the reader is presumably expected to visualize an amalgam of these juxtaposed scenes, which is neither petals nor faces, but some third image "different to both."

> The apparition of these faces in a crowd:
> Petals on a wet, black bough.

Yet, if the act of the perception of objects in juxtaposition is as the gestalt psychologists say it is, a figure / ground relationship, then it seems fair to ask whether such a synthesis of images into one image is possible. The poem might, in this respect, even remind one of the perceptual process illustrated by the equally familiar gestalt illusion:

This image (or these images) does not seem to allow for any pictorial fusion of faces and vase, merely the alternating perception of one or the other, depending on which is perceived in the foreground. The relation between the parts of Pound's poem appears to be a similarly ambiguous relation between the figure and the ground, so that one may choose to consider the faces in terms of the petals, or vice versa. Although it is evidently a poem about "faces," the use of the colon, in place of the words "are like,"[7] is what makes this ambiguity possible and gives the poem a richness it would not have if it were a simile. But can the scenes be viewed simultaneously?

Joseph Frank, in his influential essay "Spatial Form in Modern Literature," argues that Pound's definition of the image as "an intellectual and emotional complex in an instant of time" requires the poet "to overcome the inherent consecutiveness of language, frustrating the reader's normal expectation of sequence and *forcing* him to perceive the elements of the poem as juxtaposed in space rather than unrolling in time." Frank admits, however, that the "time-logic" of language conflicts with the "space-logic" of the image, and he says therefore that the understanding of such a poem "demands a complete reorientation of the reader's attitude toward language." However complete the poet's reorientation toward language might be, it was my claim in the previous chapter that the complete reorientation of the reader's attitude is not possible so long as the poems themselves make use of conventional patterns, and this poem does. The syntax of the poem, for instance, does not *force* the reader "to perceive the elements in space rather than unrolling in time," since a different temporal arrangement would produce a different effect. By playing on the convention of the simile, however, the poem may allow the reader to see more than one necessary relationship. But the dependence on syntax to create this effect undermines the idea that "simultaneity of perception," as Frank says, is made possible "by breaking up the temporal sequence."[8] The question is whether Pound's explanation, argued from his point of view as poet, that the image is an "equation" of identities and that the reader is freed from time and space limits, is adequate to describe our experience of the poem as readers.

Six Images, More or Less

With this question in mind, and considering this brief analysis of the function of comparison, I wish to turn to the six imagist poems individually, to analyze the effects which result from variations of comparative structure. Aldington's "New Love" uses the explicit comparative term *like*.

> She has new leaves
> After her dead flowers,
> Like the little almond-tree
> Which the frost hurt.

The operative comparison, however, is not the one found on either side of that term, as we might expect. The first line, in combination with the title, already contains the comparative material, in the form of a metaphor, which the *like* of the third line merely specifies. In the first line "she" is compared to a tree, and her new love to the tree's new growth of leaves. The terms of the comparison, then, are her love and the leaves, which the explicit comparison to the almond tree in the third line reiterates and reinforces. Furthermore, the new love is contrasted with the old love, by the addition of "after her dead flowers," also without benefit of the specific comparison to the frost's effect on the almond tree.

We have here, then, an explicit comparison which repeats certain implicit comparisons which are made without it. Why, we might ask, is the explicit comparison there? Despite the fact that we already know, at line two, that her new love, like new leaves, has replaced something that has died, it is not until the whole is explicitly compared to the almond tree that we know the full implication of the comparison. More than merely restating, the last two lines add specific attributes to the terms of the original comparison, allowing us to learn more about it. We learn, that is, that the subject is frail, that the dead flowers were "hurt" by some active outside agent, perhaps inevitably so. These attributes specify the subject of the poem, which is not a first love but a love tempered by hurt and loss, affected by the knowledge of change. The effect of the comparisons is to let us know what this change feels like, for they function to measure that love against changes that are known to us.

Fletcher's "The Skaters," similarly, begins with an implicit comparison and ends with the same comparison specified with *like*.

> Black swallows swooping or gliding
> In a flurry of entangled loops and curves;
> The skaters skim over the frozen river.
> And the grinding click of their skates
>   as they impinge upon the surface,
> Is like the brushing together of thin
>   wing-tips of silver.

It differs, however, in presenting the first comparison by juxtaposition, not by metaphor; that is, Fletcher says neither "the swallows skate" nor "the skaters fly," but keeps the terms of the comparison discrete by presenting them contiguously. The first comparison is less complicated than Aldington's, but no less dependent on variations on the basic convention of the simile. Whereas Aldington has kept the order of the terms consistent, for instance, Fletcher rearranges them. The subject of the first comparison, rather than being put in front, is withheld, presenting the comparison obliquely. The effect of this is to render the subject of the comparison momentarily ambiguous (even despite the title which could be read as a metaphor), whereas in Aldington's poem "she" is clearly the subject from the beginning and the reader never doubts that the poem might be about leaves rather than about her. But Fletcher's first lines, resembling in this respect the structure of Pound's "Metro" poem, begin by creating an equilibrium between the parts of the comparison, its background and foreground, thereby allowing the reader momentarily to view either swallows or skaters in terms of the other. By the end of line three, however, this delicate balance is upset, because of the grammatical relation of the two parts: *swallows* in a subordinate clause, *skaters* as the subject of the sentence. At the close of this sentence, we realize that if we were to infer a place for a *like* it would not be at the semicolon, as in the case of Pound's "Metro" couplet, but in front of the first word: "Like black swallows. . . ."

The rest of the poem affirms this relationship and outrightly compares the skaters to swallows, resolving the ambiguity and reinforcing the expectations created by the title. It is the skaters, at the end of the poem, who have been viewed in terms of the movement of the swallows, and by means of this comparison we are given a keener sense of the skater's delicate actions. But the momentary ambiguity, experienced as a result of the subtle manipulation of syntax at the beginning, has not been without purpose. The balance between the parts of the first comparison (the possibility of either term being the subject) is itself a disorienting one, considering the expected function of comparison. The reader is reoriented at the conclusion of the poem, so far as the proper subject goes, but this experience of momentary doubt, of disorientation, cannot be discounted. It is part of the poem's means. The reader feels the "entangled loops and curves" rather more immediately for having undergone the mental operation of seeking and finding the proper relationship between the terms.

The comparison in the last lines, as in Aldington's poem, does more than restate the first comparison. It adds specifically to the effect. Unlike the first figure, the terms of this comparison refer to aspects of the two experiences which are not strictly comparable. "The grinding click of their / skates as they impinge," with its force and harshness, is sufficiently incompatible with "the brushing together of thin / wing-tips" to take the reader somewhat by surprise. It informs us that the movement of the birds is not entirely smooth and harmonious, that they sometimes interfere with one another's "swooping." The two parts of the simile force an exchange of information, and the effect is to introduce an irony into the description, to suggest the harshness of the skaters as they "impinge" on the ice, crowded together. The ambiguity gives way to an ambivalence, and what the reader learns from the poem as a whole is the attitude which the speaker bears toward the subject he is describing.

H. D.'s "Oread" resembles Aldington's poem in form but is more like Fletcher's in function. Fletcher's poem is able to achieve its effect by exploiting the conventional response to the simile. That is, it is only because we expect a comparative relationship to function by viewing one thing in terms of another that the poem is able to fool us momentarily, and to switch our perspective from swallows in terms of skaters to skaters in terms of swallows, or at least to make us wonder briefly which it is. H. D.'s poem makes similar use of the same expectation.

> Whirl up, sea—
> whirl your pointed pines,
> splash your great pines
> on our rocks,
> hurl your green over us
> cover us with your pools of fir.

There are no explicit comparisons in the poem, only those made implicitly by the substitution of a word from one category of experience to refer to something in another category. The reader, on reaching the second line of the poem, is asked to consider some aspect of the sea which is like pines, and the structure is comparative in this sense, like Aldington's opening lines. With the third line we learn that that aspect is waves, and a perfect analogy is set up, which the rest of the poem maintains and specifies, between ocean waves and pines. Although the analogy is self-evident, the reader is put in much the same situation as at the beginning of Fletcher's poem, and in this case the syntax does little to help reorient the reader's perspective. That is, the lack of any place to infer a *like*, and the poet's suppression of explicit comparison, renders the two terms of the comparison interchangeable. The poem is ambiguous throughout, then, in the same manner in which Fletcher's poem begins. The reader is uncertain whether it is the sea in terms of the forest, or vice versa. The first line might cause us to think that the sea is the subject of the comparison, because it is mentioned first, but a moment's reflection is sufficient to change one's perspective enough for it to be the forest. It is a matter of which words one decides to take literally. If the forest is being compared to the sea, *sea* and *splash* become metaphors, and *pines* is literal. If the sea is the subject of the comparison, *pines* becomes the metaphor, *sea* becomes literal. It is not possible, however, to conceive of them as both literal and metaphoric at the same time. Like that optical illusion, then, the poem can change before our very eyes, so to speak, and certainly this is a substantial part of its overall effect.

The poem is a plea from an Oread, a mountain nymph. To whom is it a plea? A mountain nymph would be expected to refer to the effects of the sea *as if* they were effects of the forest. And yet, seeking the proper metaphor for her home, a mountain nymph might as easily refer to the effects of the forest *as if* they were effects of the sea. For what is it a plea? If she is speaking to the sea, it seems she is pleading for destruction. If she is speaking to the forest, it seems to be a plea for some sort of security. To the degree that it is a plea *to* either, so it is a plea *for* either, and at that point the poet leaves us to ponder. The critic Hugh Witemeyer has paraphrased this plea in terms which capture this paradoxical quality—a "desire for pleasant obliteration"[9]—without, however, accounting for this effect in the uses to which comparative strategies are put.

The comparative material in Pound's "Liu Ch'e," by contrast, is subordinated, and yet it is situated in the poem so as to make it central to the poem's effect.

> The rustling of the silk is discontinued,
> Dust drifts over the court-yard,
> There is no sound of foot-fall, and the leaves
> Scurry into heaps and lie still,
> And she the rejoicer of the heart is beneath them:
>
> A wet leaf that clings to the threshold.

The first four lines are descriptive, and contain neither metaphor nor explicit comparison. They do use metonymy, however, to give the sense that some activity has just been completed, for the details of the description refer to what is no more or to what is just entering to replace some previously human activity. Rustling of silk is replaced by dust, footfalls by leaves, activity by stillness. These lines are completed by a fifth line of description, in which metonymy is no longer present. It seems to be a literal statement. At this point, however, ambiguities are allowed to come into the description. "And she the rejoicer of the heart is beneath them." If "she" is the cause of the activity which has just been replaced by stillness, which we might assume to be the case, then what does it mean to say she is "beneath them"? Beneath what? Beneath in what sense? Does it mean that she is dead and buried beneath the leaves in the courtyard? Or does it mean that she feels beneath them, that her power to make the heart rejoice, or her dignity somehow, is beneath theirs? There are other possibilities. The reader hopes that the final line might clarify, at least. At this juncture we find Pound's characteristic colon, the signal that what follows is to be "equated" with what has come before. What follows is a comparison, made, like Fletcher's, by juxtaposition. She is *like* "a wet leaf that clings to the threshold." But this comparison does not resolve the ambiguity in the previous line; it only compounds it. If she is dead, then the comparison serves to tell us how the speaker feels. He compares her to the leaf to inform us of the poignancy of his grief, perhaps, the threshold representing the frame of his consciousness, the tangibility of her recent memory and the intangibility of her recent loss. If, however, the other meaning of *beneath* is recalled, then the comparison functions to inform us about how *she* feels, *i.e.* unwilling, because reticent, to enter (or to leave) the scene in which the other leaves scurry and lie still. The essential ambiguity of the fifth line, therefore, renders the whole of the imagistic comparison equivocal, in that it might be said to be an "equation" for the emotions of either the speaker of the poem or of its subject.

With this conclusion in mind, it is interesting and productive to compare the poem with another English version of the same Chinese original, the version from which Pound apparently worked, that of Herbert Giles:

> The sound of rustling silk is stilled,
> With dust the marble courtyard filled;
> No footfalls echo on the floor,
> Fallen leaves in heaps block up the door. . . .
> For she, my pride, my lovely one, is lost,
> And I am left, in hopeless anguish tossed,

In comparing these poems, Hugh Witemeyer says, "With his un-rhymed *vers libre*, Pound avoids the metrical monotony of Giles's couplets; and with his concrete image of the wet leaf, he gives a far more powerful equation for sorrow than Giles's rhetorical inversion, 'In hopeless anguish tossed'."[10] Certainly the critic is taking advantage of the opportunity for hindsight. Pound's version allows the possibility that the image renders the speaker's anguish, but, because it allows for other possibilities as well, it renders this emotion with less certainty than does Giles's poem. By taking the poem to be a direct translation, Witemeyer fails to notice that Pound must equate the clinging leaf with the speaker, whereas in his version it is not "I" who is left. By substituting the concrete "image" for the abstract name of the emotion, Pound has created an ambiguity which is not found in Giles's version. He may have found the phrase "hopeless anguish" vague, but his own version replaces this vagueness with an uncertainty. If it was meant to correct Giles's failure to communicate the precise emotion of the speaker, then we must conclude that it fails to do so, since it is only by reference to Giles's poem that we can resolve with any certainty *what* and *whose* emotion is being presented. Having done so we might well conclude that the poem is more "powerful." It seems that we might better account for Pound's transformation of this poem as an attempt to take the emotion away from the speaker, or the subject, and to fix it, somehow, in the scene.

Allen Upward's "The Sea Shell" comes from a collection with a similar Oriental emphasis, "Scented Leaves from a Chinese Jar," which is not made up of translations, however, but attempts to duplicate the effects of Chinese forms.

> To the passionate lover, whose sighs
> come back to him on every breeze, all
> the world is like a murmuring sea-shell.

It too, like Pound's poem, uses the strategy of comparison in order to give concreteness to an emotion. Unlike Pound's poem, it does not suppress the abstract emotional term, but tells us outright that the lover is "passionate." The effect of this is that the emotion which is rendered by comparison is not as equivocal. Perhaps, in this, the poem violates imagist doctrine: Don't mix "an abstraction with the concrete. . . . It dulls the image. . . . Go in fear of abstractions."[11] But, however much it depends on abstraction, the poem is a clear presentation of an emotion. In this instance the comparison is used differently from those in the other poems we have seen, however, because the emotion is as clearly portrayed in the beginning of the poem, "To the passionate lover, whose sighs come back to him on every breeze," as it is in the comparison, "all the world is like a murmuring sea-shell." The function of the comparison is not to specify that emotion for us. Rather than signifying *what* the emotion is, the comparison serves to render the *degree* of the emotion. "A murmuring sea-shell" might be interesting for a while, but its mere monotony, its predictability, causes it to be quickly abandoned. The sound of the sea in a conch may have a compelling force to it; it may hold out a promise of some sort, yet it is also ultimately disappointing in its unreality. We are meant to think of this sound, not as significant, but as a sort of inarticulate noise, which, if it were "all the world" would be hopelessly unsatisfying. Such are the attributes, at least, that Upward seems to have brought to the comparison. These associations are not made arbitrarily. They result from the reader's attempt to deal with the demands of comparative structure, to isolate attributes of each category which may be shared by both. By means of these attributes we understand more precisely what the lover's passion feels like, and the attributes of the sea shell, transferred to the state of longing, become significant of the degree of that longing.

Amy Lowell's "The Fisherman's Wife" is imagistic in that it uses natural or physical details as the verbal "equivalent" of emotion.

> When I am alone,
> The wind in the pine trees

> Is like the shuffling of waves
> Upon the wooden sides of a boat.

The way in which it presents emotion through a selection of such details, however, is not precisely the way that imagist theory required. The rules of imagism, if followed literally, obliged the poet to condense so radically that the obliqueness of the communication alone renders it ambiguous, as in the case of Pound's "Liu Ch'e." Upward escaped ambiguity by using the abstract adjective "passionate," which he ought, perhaps, to have eschewed to make his poem conform to imagist prescriptions. Lowell's device for avoiding the ambiguity inherent in these prescriptions was less obviously a violation of a technical imagist principle, and in fact seems to follow from the further requirement that the imagist poet be objective: She has conveyed the nature of the emotion by putting the words of her poem into the voice of a fictional speaker and created a dramatic situation which clearly occasions that speaker's words. There is no pretense that it is the poet's own emotion that is being presented. H. D. in her "Oread" had done something similar, but she had withheld the specific sorts of information that allow us to identify the dramatic motivation of Lowell's speaker. Thus, "Oread" continues to be an oblique presentation of emotion. "The Fisherman's Wife" does not allow the reader to misconstrue the speaker's feelings. The reader is guided by the title and the first line to conclude that the woman is speaking out of a state of separation and loneliness.

The comparison that follows, between the wind in the pines and the waves on the side of the boat, functions to measure the intensity of that loneliness for us, in the same way that the comparison in Upward's poem functions to measure the feeling otherwise identified. Because we apprehend this comparison through the speaker's point of view, the simile might be said to be more direct than Upward's, less of a mere illustration. The terms of Lowell's comparison inform us that the wife cannot see her own world in terms other than of her absent husband's world, and her loneliness therefore is a type of empathy rather than self-pity. As long as the husband is away, she too is at sea. They are together, in fact, insofar as she perceives her own surroundings in terms of his. This is the loneliness that is nearly a comfort, or, it is the loneliness that can be endured because her pain is in her feeling of closeness. Lowell has used the reader's expectations of the stereotype of the lonely wife to tell us something about the nature of that special loneliness which is not commonplace. To create such an effect is one of the ends of imagism—to see the unique emotion apart from the conventional—but the prescribed means of imagism do not include the use of such a fictional speaker. In other words, as long as the speaker is obviously a persona, the reader cannot make the direct connection to the poet's unique experience which imagism called for. Such a distant persona achieves the illusion of direct-ness, only.

Images and Critical Method

The first thing we may notice about the foregoing analyses, as I have already suggested, is that the isolation of the comparative functions did not depend on our ability to see, in the mind's eye, the physical objects that were named. At least this visualization played no part in the description of these functions. We may have had such images or we may not. The fact that we were able to visualize a scene in our minds did not contribute to our under-standing of the intended effect of the poem, so long as we hold to our conception of "intended" as that end which accounts for the means of the poem, as we must do from our limited perspective as readers. No other intention but this implicit one, this reconstruc-table one, is available to us. Thus, the poems were able to control our experience of the comparisons whereas they were only able to occasion our experience of some mental image. Hence, our visual response is irrelevant to an attempt to account for the means which the poem employs.

Thus, to return to Hulme's test: We cannot know, when con-fronted by the poem, whether there was a physical object which the poet actually saw and in which he delighted, nor could it pos-sibly make any difference. The reason lies in the very choice of words as the medium, and the effect which they have as opposed to the effect of a visual medium such as sculpture. The graphic arts deal in particularity (even the nonrepresentational forms of graphic art) in the sense that the forms or objects which are presented to the viewer are perceived as uniquely themselves. Words, insofar as they refer to such unique objects of sense perception, cannot convey the uniqueness of the object and suffice only to place it within a class of similar objects. In this sense, words, inevitably, name abstractions.[12] However narrow the class to which a word refers, there are within it many possible variations on the object, all named by the word. Additional words, such as adjectives (or passages of minute description) may serve to narrow the class, but the degree to which they can approach a determinate description is always limited. (The poems we have seen make no attempt to use adjectives or additional words to achieve greater detail; to do so was forbidden by imagist theory in the interest of economy.) The reader, as opposed to the viewer of a sculpture, is always faced with indeterminate possibilities which, if the object is re-created in the mind's eye as an image, will be completed without reference to the clues (*i.e.* controls) given by the actual words. The indeterminate possibilities left open by words will be filled in by attributes from the reader's unique imagination, not by attributes which are necessarily part of the object that the poet names. "A mental image," writes P. N. Furbank,

> is no less and no more than what you put there. You can never learn anything from mental images, since they are merely a way of presenting to yourself what you already know. . . . You can never stand back and scrutinise a mental image, since you are fully occupied in creating it—it represents your consciousness in action. If you imagine St. Paul's Cathedral to yourself you cannot *count* the columns of the portico, to see how many there are, for it is entirely up to you how many you put there. . . . Forming mental pictures is not perceiving or observing a real copy (more or less lifelike) of an external object; it is performing a playful imitation of a man perceiving something.[13]

The reader who visualizes a written description, or a figure, in a poem is having an imitative experience of this sort, even though the poet may have had an experience of a different sort, *i.e.* of

finding words to describe what he observed in a real object. But if
the poet had described an object dimly recollected, or wholly in-
vented, the same poem, in the same language, could have just as
easily resulted. The reader is in no position to decide which it is,
and for this reason Hulme's test for poetry is impossible to apply.

It is crucial to remember about any imagist discussion of "ac-
curate presentation" or the necessity of finding the "exact word,"
even if it does not apply exclusively to visual sense perceptions,
that such things are being argued from the poet's point of view
rather than the reader's. That is, although the imagists held that
the poet must find a means of capturing and rendering a sensation
exactly as perceived, one cannot appeal to this same principle to
account for the reader's experience of the poem. Even if the poet
has attempted to render the exact sensation, the reader is inevita-
bly confronted with words, words to which the adjective *exact* ap-
plies only relatively because they lack the power to reproduce
those sensations in all their uniqueness. Only the poet can judge
their "exactness." The attempt by readers to do so, insofar as they
would make the conversion from prescriptive imagist poetics to a
theory of how to read imagist poems, is misconceived. Not only
will the reader never know whether the mental image that he con-
jures up is the one that the poet is attempting to describe, but he
will be reproducing every poem after his own image, so to speak.

If the reader attempts to make the poem a point of departure
for the creation of visual experience, he has admitted, in effect,
that the poet has surrendered control over his experience of the
poem. Since the precise visual images produced in the reader's
imagination will be a reflection, not of the poet's, but of the
reader's own previous experience with physical sensations, the
poet is assumed to have created no more than an arbitrary stim-
ulus. As I said above, poems may occasion such mental images,
but their power to control them is limited. What may be con-
trolled by poems, from the reader's point of view, is the cognitive
experience of the patterns made by the words that are presented,
for readers competent in the conventions appealed to by the pat-
terns. In this sense, the patterns of language, for the reader, are
temporal *events*. The pattern of comparison controls one such

event, the conventional response to which is to associate attributes of semantic categories. By means of this controlled experience the reader is made to learn something which he himself has not invented. Furbank also writes that "analogies in literature are never *just* analogies. They are also words in a certain order, producing dynamic effects through their logical associations, through their syntax, and through all sorts of rhythmic, acoustic and mimetic qualities." [14] All such qualities contribute to the reader's experience. It must be granted that these functions are often more difficult to describe analytically than visual impressions, but they are finally more important. The term *image* has been used to refer to all of these functions and more, thus compounding the difficulty by drawing the reader's attention away from such controlled aspects of the text to its uncontrolled aspects.

It is necessary, then, to be cautious and even somewhat skeptical about the critical uses to which this word *image* may be put. Modern attempts to define *image*, such as "a mental picture evoked by the use of metaphors, similes, and other figures of speech," or "the representation in poetry of any sense experience," seem to conflate otherwise useful categories, in that they refer to a psychology of response without having the power to distinguish functional operations within the poem. We would not have to stretch the meaning of *image* to include "*any* sense experience," illogically, if we could escape our dependence on the word itself as a substitute for the many, various operations that can be performed with words. Such definitions seem more to result from attempts to justify a term already in extravagant use—"to mean anything mentioned by the poet," as Christine Brooke-Rose has put it—than to create a critically useful category. Or, a definition of *image* such as Hugh Kenner's "what the words actually name," [15] might signify the critic's acceptance of the metaphysical assumptions concerning the underlying unity of word-thing-emotion implied by imagist theory.

J. V. Cunningham is among the few critics who have pointed out the danger of the implication of such definitions that all figures of speech have a corresponding mental image. A figure, he says, is like a "conceit," in that it is a "piece of wit," a mental process. He

illustrates: "There is about as much of an image in 'Till the con-
version of the Jews,' as there would be in 'till the cows come
home,' and it would be a psychiatrically sensitive reader who
would immediately visualize the lowing herd winding slowly o'er
the lea." The risk taken by an all-inclusive definition of *image* is
that we make such sensitive and impressionistic readers, compell-
ing them to respond visually to every turn of phrase, whether or
not such a response is appropriate to the meaning of the poem,
and to attribute this response to the intention of the poet. The po-
tential for misreadings is obvious. The problem is to decide if the
effect of a particular phrase is, as Josephine Miles puts it, "basically
sensuous or basically comparative,"[16] and the solution seems to be
to ask what effects the phrasings in the poem may control, given
the conventions of language. If the subject of critical inquiry is
function, we have to look for explanations of poetic effects in pro-
cesses which are capable of being controlled by the language of the
poem. The concept of a figure of speech as a structure of thought
rather than a sensual stimulus allows us to do just this. The dif-
ference between "image" as a structure and "image" as a picture,
then, lies simply in the degree to which the reader's response re-
sults from controllable or uncontrollable processes. We might re-
serve the word *image* for appeals to conventional pictorial re-
sponses, in the way the Renaissance rhetoricians used the term
Icon to refer to representations in words of pictures already famil-
iar to the audience.

The experience of poetic events is conveyed, in the words of
Donald Davie, because "the sentence enacts the thing it says."
Recognizing the danger in such an explanation of generating an
impressionism of its own, we can understand it to refer simply to
the sort of experience that is derived from the syntax of a poem, as
in the previous analyses of imagist poems. Our response to these
poems could not literally be said to have been the result of being
freed from "time limits and space limits" (as Pound's definition
of the image requires), nor were we prevented from "gliding
through an abstract process" (as Hulme maintained we must be).
The construction of poems into syntactic patterns in fact encour-
ages us to undergo a process of temporal sequence, and the effect

of the poem depends on our doing so. Pound's idea that the image occurs "in an instant of time" has been called untenable by Walter Sutton "because it is inconsistent with the organic nature of the reading process, which involves the gradual and tentative apprehension of the form of a complex and many sided phenomenon in a shifting time perspective."[17] Thus, the syntactic shifts of Fletcher's poem, for example, are not arbitrary; they "enact" a process which is undergone by the reader, and that enactment is meaningful.

Thus, if we had discussed the visual effects which the poems are capable of stimulating, we would have been farther from knowing the meaning of the poems. If we had lingered, for example, over the word "almond" in Aldington's poem, in an effort to reconstruct the mental image of our memory of an almond tree as opposed to some other sort of tree, our attention would have been misdirected, and our experience of the poem would have been led away from the emotion which the poem seems designed to convey. If we had sought, in other words, the essence of "almondness"—directed perhaps by Fenollosa's discussion of "cherryness"[18]—we would have been farther from knowing what was essential about the "new love." In fact, it makes little difference, in this poem, whether it is an almond tree or, say, a peach tree, *except* insofar as we know almond trees to have attributes which are uniquely capable of affecting our understanding of the new love being described. The fact that it is an almond tree might be said to alter our understanding of the degree of the experience, insofar as almond trees are, say, particularly frail. But the smallness and vulnerability which we associate with the almond tree are cognitive attributes, and remain so whether we visualize a tree or not. The nature of the emotion is made apparent to us by the movement from the implicit comparison, and the changes which this movement forces on our attention.

Similarly, in H. D.'s poem, should we have lingered over the fact that the "fir" is the type of pine which is named, we would have been led astray. Certainly the word itself is an important part of the function of the poem, for to end the poem, which has spoken only of "pines" in general, with the name of a particular kind of pine makes the Oread's plea more immediate. But rather than ask ourselves what a "fir" looks like (for it can look like any number of different firs) or what sensations it evokes (which depend more upon us than on the word), in an attempt to find some description which would be equivalent to sensations in the mind of the poet, we should ask ourselves what, in the context of the poem, would have caused the Oread to find the specific name suddenly more appropriate than the generic. The movement from general to particular forces the reader to follow the Oread as her perception changes. Any other type of pine, bearing the same relation to the general category, would have had the same effect, *i.e.* to render the movement of the persona's mind as the plea becomes more emphatic and the effect more immediate. If one assumes that the reader is supposed to "image" a fir tree, as opposed to all other types of pine, it is further assumed that the poet expects the reader to know the morphological differences between a fir and, say, a spruce. (Is it a balsam fir or a silver fir? *Fir* itself is generic.) In what way could it possibly matter, considering the context of the poem? In fact, it is probably only in terms of prosody, or perhaps as a pun, that one should consider the appropriateness of this particular term.

In the poems I have examined, the degree of dependence on syntax was a matter of how much the structure departed from an expected, conventional comparative structure, and syntax played a role of moving the reader through the experience of the poem, therefore, to the degree that the reader was made to feel the departure from the norm. Such a feeling, I have contended, is consistent with the meaning of the poem. Yet the feeling which results from the experience of the figure is not the same as the emotion being described. It does, however, function by providing information about that emotion. Thus, Davie speaks of syntax as moving a reader "by the fidelity with which it follows a *form* of action," much as Suzanne Langer has spoken of poetic structure as communicating the morphology of feeling, or "what it feels like to feel." Similarly, J. V. Cunningham says that poetic structure provides the reader with "the experience of having experienced."[19] These critics have had to depend on figures themselves to explain that analogy communicates a feeling which is distinct from the experience of the emotions in the poem, yet which is fundamental to its communication because morphologically like it. Analogy, after all, is not a literal appeal, and there is no reason that it should make sense at all except for its power to move the reader through a process of thought.

Based on what has been said so far, we can isolate two related methodological problems in imagist theory, if that theory is taken out of the poet's point of view in which it is argued and made into a manner of reading. I have already alluded to them. Adopting the ways of the literary theoreticians, we might be justified now in presenting them as "fallacies."

The *fallacy of reciprocity* (for lack of a more elegant term) is the notion that, having associated an emotion with a sensible object, one is able to communicate that emotion by means of the words which describe the object. Such an idea results from the imagists' desire for "direct" communication through intuition. From the poet's point of view it is an attempt to bring language closer to the realities of perception, and to deal with the perceivable fact that "things" sometimes affect us emotionally. If the imagist concept of poetic communication—that an object causes an emotion which is stimulated in the reader by an image of the object—is applied as a method of reading, it must be assumed that the reader can (and will) feel the same emotion that the poet felt, reciprocally, with no other aid than the description of the object. Thus, it is further assumed that the emotional effect of "things" is among their inherent attributes, rather than a function of the perceiver.

This assumed reciprocal mechanism has been refuted by Kenneth Burke, who offers his reason, here, by analogy to the difficulty of communicating the unique emotions of dreams: "at times we look back on the dream and are mystified at the seemingly unwarranted emotional responses which the details 'aroused' in us. Trying to convey to others the emotional overtones of this dream, we laboriously recite the details, and are compelled at every turn to put in such confessions of defeat as 'There was something strange about the room,' or, 'For some reason or other I was afraid of this boat, although there doesn't seem to be any good reason now.' *But the details were not the cause of the emotion; the emotion, rather, dictated the selection of the details.*" Just so in our emotional reaction to things, and our attempts to communicate them: Our perceptions of feeling are not a function of the objects, which only seem to cause them, but a function of our own state of receptivity. Thus, Burke provides the reason that an image alone is insufficient to control an emotion in a reader which is equivalent to that felt by the poet who selected the image. Emotions are communicable, rather, says Burke, by finding a formal means of "externalizing the sense of crescendo," for example, or making use of some other "condition of appeal," which results *in* the emotion rather than *from* it. The effect is controllable, as Burke points out, because such patterns come to poetry from conventional discourse, paralleling processes found in language elsewhere. Burke says of conventions that they "exercize formal potentialities of the reader. They enable the mind to follow processes amenable to it. . . . The forms of art . . . can be said to have a prior existence in the experiences of the person hearing or reading the work of art. They parallel processes which characterize his experiences outside of art."[20]

The imagists were well aware that single words, or simple descriptions, have no such power to communicate emotions. This, indeed, is one of the aspects of language they sought to overcome. They created the theory of the image as the juxtaposition of two such descriptions in an effort to break the conventional, "amenable" responses to language which they thought to prevent direct, intuitive communication. The image proper was therefore not a single "word picture," but two. In his essay "Vorticism," Pound said that "the image is itself the speech. The image is the word beyond formulated language." Yet the juxtaposition of images was a formula. He went on to address the question of how to formulate the image, in the manner of the sculptor or painter:

> The pine-tree in mist upon the far hill looks like a fragment of Japanese armour.
> The beauty of this pine-tree in the mist is not caused by its resemblance to the plates of the armour.
> . . . The beauty, in so far as it is beauty of form, is the result of "planes in relation."

The tree and the armour are beautiful because their diverse planes overlie in a certain manner.

There is the sculptor's or the painter's *key*. The presentation of this beauty is primarily his job. And the "poet"? "Pourquoi doubler l'image?" asks [Henri-Martin] Barzun in declaiming against this "poesie farcie de 'comme.'" The poet, whatever his "figure of speech," will not arrive by doubling or confusing an image.

Still, the artist, working in words only, may cast on the reader's mind a more vivid image of either the armour or the pine by mentioning them close together or by using some device of simile or metaphor, that is a legitimate procedure of his art, for he works not with planes or with colours but with the names of objects and of properties.

Thus, despite his objection a few pages earlier in the essay to the "rhetorical habit" of "defining things always 'in terms of something else,'" Pound here conceded that the poet may legitimately create similes and metaphors as a means of bringing the image into prominence, because of the nature of words. He did so reluctantly, it seems, for his sympathies lay with Barzun against this "poesie farcie de 'comme.'" The combination of two descriptions, bringing out their relations, was thought to be capable of achieving the effect which one description could not, and so even the simile was sanctioned as an imagist technique, despite its evident "rhetorical" nature, so long as it did not "confuse the image." But in fact, such a combination *was* the image. In 1916, the editors of *Some Imagist Poets* said, "The 'exact' word does not mean the word which exactly describes the object in itself, it means the 'exact' word which brings the effect of that object before the reader as it presented itself to the poet's mind at the time of writing the poem. Imagists deal but little in similes although much of their poetry is metaphorical. The reason for this is that while acknowledging the figure to be an integral part of all poetry, they feel that the constant imposing of one figure upon another in the same poem blurs the central effect."[21] The quotation marks around *exact* here, are a sign of the imagists' inconsistent attitude toward the word as a vehicle for bringing "the effect of the object before the reader." Despite what they said here, the poets dealt heavily in similes. The poet's emotion may have been stimulated by a single scene or object (as

Pound's emotion was stimulated by the faces in the Metro station only, not by petals), but in order to create the formulation of the emotion the poet sought to find a second scene or object to which to relate the first.

The fallacy of accident here presents itself. Because Hulme thought that language must resist convention in order to become intuitive, he wanted the image to present an "unlooked-for resemblance." Only when the emotion occurred to the poet without his seeking it could the poet be assured of having escaped a stereotyped process. But if the image is the verbal formula for the emotion, then it can hardly be the same emotion which is stimulated by one half of the formula. T. S. Eliot exemplified this fallacy, by arguing, in "The Metaphysical Poets," that the conceit (like the image) forces disparate ideas together to create a sudden unity and that this unity is equivalent to the state of mind which is being expressed. If the new unity, however, is in fact new, and in fact sudden, then it cannot be said to be equivalent to the state which stimulated the poet's search for "the verbal equivalent" in which to communicate it. Similarly, if the juxtaposition of images produces a new meaning, then that meaning could not logically have existed prior to the creation of the juxtaposition. An imagist apologist illustrates precisely the logical problem of such thinking: "In poetry, different elements of experience, different kinds of thoughts and emotions, find a harmonious synthesis and *a meaning in combination which they did not have before the poet brought them together*," writes A. R. Jones. He goes on, however, to say that "the reading of poetry is an act of cooperation between poet and reader in which the reader, by virtue of poetic imagery shaped under the immediate pressure of reality, is able to seize *the poet's original intuition*."[22] I have brought these two passages together to illustrate the danger, once again, of using the prescriptive point of view of the poet to explain the reader's experience. The two emphasized phrases cannot logically coexist. The poet is presumed to have known what the new meaning was before the juxtaposition of images was found which uniquely creates it. Either one feels an emotion and *seeks* for a proper way to communicate it, or one comes across an *unsought* resemblance which has no connection with one's "*original* intuition." In either case, there is no way for the reader to know which it was. The reader can no more decide if the poem resulted from a purposeful or from an accidental combination, than he can tell if the combination presents precisely the emotion which the poet felt. One cannot know these things any more than one can know what object the poet actually saw, and in none of these cases should it make a difference in the reader's experience of the poem.

These criteria of imagist theory, then, are often irrelevant to the reader's task, whatever else they may be to the poet. What is at issue in reading an imagistic poem is not how one re-creates the poet's emotions or experience, based on inadequate evidence, but how one responds to the formal strategies of the poem. The persistent notion of the image as a special device for rendering the poet's unique emotion through sensual evocation allows the reader to neglect the fact that imagist poems are constructed like many other sorts of poems, that they have more in common with other kinds of poems than is apparent from the reformist stance of their poetics, and that their interpretation depends more on what they have in common with other kinds of poetry than on how they differ. As far as the "image" itself is concerned, the strategy in question is the use of comparison as a figure of speech.

Josephine Miles has said that "metaphor . . . trades upon relations in categories. That is, it trades upon common, rather than uncommon, word-association patterns."[23] To associate two words in relations which their lexical usages do not ordinarily permit, or to substitute a figuratively used word for a literal concept, creates tension. There is, in any such relation of words, similarity and difference, and it is the sense of difference which makes the language metaphoric. It is the similarity, however, which gives it meaning. This is the point of Miles's distinction between common and uncommon word-association patterns. The words *common* and *uncommon* have two references here. One is to the attributes which the categories named by the related words share or do not share. The meaning of a metaphor is to be found in what they share, although the intensity of that meaning depends on the degree of tension created by what they do not. The other meaning of *com-*

mon and *uncommon* is in reference to the reader. Without the shared sense of similarity between the parts of a metaphor, shared, that is, on the part of the reader and the poet, no sense can be made of it. It is in this sense that the word *pattern* becomes relevant. Patterns are only patterns if they are recognized as such, and the basis of this recognition is to be found in the reader's experience with similar patterns and the basis of their use is in the author's assumption that the reader will have such a recognition.

Thus, the use of figurative language implies a link to an audience, no less so than "ordinary" language does. Donald Davie speaks of the language of poetry in terms that express this link: "What is in question plainly is a sort of contract entered into tacitly by speaker and hearer, writer and reader; a convention which both observe. This would be anathema to Fenollosa, for whom the only contract the poet should honour is that between himself and 'nature'. Hulme goes further and says that the contracts normally in being between speaker and hearer are only a hindrance to the poet." [24] The imagist's way of thinking indeed requires that the poet assume no responsibility to keep a "contract" with the reader, because he cannot acknowledge that one exists. The "direct communication" which Hulme sought through intuitive responses requires the breaking of the conventional "contract" that language ordinarily requires. What Davie is getting at, and what I would like to expand on briefly, is that the very use of figures of speech involves a "contractual" agreement. In particular, the use of analogy depends on the poet's carrying out an agreement to use similarities which are recognizable on the basis of the reader's assumed experience.

Thus, when Richard Aldington writes "She has new leaves / After her dead flowers," he has agreed to acknowledge that the reader has had a certain experience which can be drawn on to lead the reader to an understanding of some experience which he has not had. The reader is assumed to have something in common with the poet, which the poet can use to lead the reader to know something which they do *not* share. The new love, in this case, is the unshared, or uncommon, experience, the one that the poet wishes to communicate. The term chosen for the analogy is the shared experience, and thus it can be used to communicate, on the basis of its common attributes, something unique about the new love, not previously known. We know what the new love is like, therefore, precisely because we know already what trees, leaves, and flowers are like, and the poet has used the assumption that we do know to lead us to the new apprehension.

The function of figurative language, then, is to convey information. The only information about emotions which can be put into language (beyond giving them abstract names or relatively less abstract adjectives: "intense sorrow") is to say what they feel *like*. To convey information of this experiential sort, the poet must assume the reader to know something, to have felt something, in the first place.

There is always, then, a *thing compared* and a *thing compared to*, in imagist poetry, the first being the experience which the reader and the poet do not share, and the second being the comparable experience which they do share and which permits them to share something of the first. It is part of the poet's "contract" with the reader to use shared experience as the *thing compared to*, and this is why Miles has written that metaphor "trades upon *common*, rather than uncommon" patterns. A figure of speech, then, has a subject, and it has comparative material. Many terms have been devised to identify these components. I. A. Richards has given us *tenor* and *vehicle*. It is occasionally more illuminating to use the terms of gestalt psychology, *figure* and *ground*, because they, unlike Richards' terms, identify functions within the reader rather than within the text, *i.e.* of response rather than semantic structure alone.

The imagists, as we have already seen, often deliberately confused the figure and the ground, as in Pound's "Metro," Fletcher's "The Skaters" and, most effectively, H. D.'s "Oread." They did so for a reason. "Metaphor," said Fenollosa, is "the revealer of nature."[25] The poem, in other words, by directly embodying nature's truth, illuminates nature's intentions. Such a conception of metaphor reverses the relationship one would ordinarily expect to obtain. We would ordinarily expect, that is, our knowledge of nature to reveal the intentional, human meanings of metaphors. To reverse the *thing compared to* and the *thing compared*—to render the figure and ground ambiguous—is a special device of imagism, the function of which is to promote a belief in the harmony of words and things. In ambiguous patterns the figure and ground are interchangeable. Such patterns make one of the ways that the convention of comparative structure can be used to convince a reader that an order prevails, a unity between the parallel spheres of *res* and *verba*. It is a device of rhetoric, then, in the sense spoken of by Wallace Stevens.

Three Uses of Comparison

The uses of comparative strategy can be seen throughout the poetry of the imagists, and we turn now to that poetry once again. We have already seen three ways in which comparative structures are formed in imagist poems: by metaphor, by explicit comparison, and by juxtaposition. But certain distinctions of function overlap these categories, and I would like now to consider how the imagists used three types of comparison based, not on form or material, but on function. They are: 1) the comparison of *attributes* in which the emotion is specified for the reader, 2) the comparison of *degree* in which the intensity of the emotion is measured for the reader, and 3) comparison as a form of *induction* in which examples are used as evidence of the plausibility of certain emotions.

The first function to be discussed, then, is that of comparison of attributes in order to specify an emotion. Consider the following poem by Richard Aldington, "October":

> The beech-leaves are silver
> For lack of the tree's blood.
>
> At your kiss my lips
> Become like the autumn beech-leaves.

In the first two lines the poet gives us information about the leaves, which, when they are compared to the state of the poet, become information about that state. The analogy is straightfor-ward. What is true of the leaves is true of the speaker's lips, and the poet's comparison is thus a means of informing the reader about what the kiss feels like. What is true of the leaves? They are also presented in figurative terms. They lack "blood," a simple sub-stitution for "color," perhaps, but having attributes such as "life force." Our conclusion, based on the information presented, is that the kiss seems to steal the blood from the speaker's lips, that there is something life-denying about it. The experience of the speaker is not that usually associated with a kiss, and yet in the comparison to the beech-leaves this somewhat negative connota-tion is rendered natural.

The most characteristically imagist form of comparison, more like Pound's third-person "Metro" poem than like Aldington's first-person "October," is the juxtaposition of two short descrip-tions, as in Lowell's "The Pond":

> Cold, wet leaves
> Floating on moss-coloured water,
> And the croaking of frogs—
> Cracked bell-notes in the twilight.

In such cases the emotion is conveyed obliquely, and because of both the form and the subject chosen for comparison, it is nearly always the same emotion: an awed reverence, or a meditative thrill. The means by which the emotion is understood is the way in which the juxtaposition forces the reader to account for a state of mind which could call such perceptions forth. In the first de-scription, apparently, lies the observation, and in the second lies the poet's attempt to show the effect of that observation by means of the imaginative association it creates. As long as no reference is made to that state of mind, the communication seems to depend on the reader's ability to see the appropriateness of the transition. One reason this mode of presentation can be said to result in the same emotion over and over, then, is because it appeals to the reader's sense of being in the same frame of mind as the poet, and this sense of identification predominates over any actual involvement in the details of the scene. The two parts of H. D.'s "Storm" present the reader with two such comparisons:

I

You crash over the trees,
you crack the live branch:
the branch is white,
the green crushed,
each leaf is rent like split wood.

II

You burden the trees
with black drops,
you swirl and crash:
you have broken off a weighted leaf
in the wind—
it is hurled out,
whirls up and sinks,
a green stone.

The meditative thrill is rendered here in much the same way, first through an explicit and then through an implicit comparison. If there is a difference in the nature of the two emotions being communicated, it seems to be the result of the relative appropriateness of the two terms chosen as comparative material in each case. "Split wood," is drawn from the context of the observation itself; it is such a term as might be chosen by someone meditating on the indiscriminatory violence of the storm. "A green stone," however, although an appropriate comparative term to communicate the effect of the dropping leaves, is drawn from outside the context of the observation, and it compels the reader to be more aware of the speaker's state of mind, to be drawn more into that state to account for the choice of this term. The second is the more "imagistic" technique. In a rudimentary form, Hulme was playing with such a technique in "Above the Dock":

Above the quiet dock in midnight,
Tangled in the tall mast's corded height,
Hangs the moon. What seemed so far away
Is but a child's balloon, forgotten after play.

Render this poem in free verse ("strip it of rhetoric," as Flint would say) and you would have an imagist haiku, something, perhaps, like:

> The moon,
> Tangled in the corded masts:
> A child's balloon, forgotten.

Similarly, a poem by Edward Storer called "Image," from a collection which Flint cited as "the first books of 'Imagist' poems,"[26] is a comparative construction of this sort:

> Forsaken lovers,
> Burning to a chaste white moon,
> Upon strange pyres of loneliness and drought.

To render this poem in the later imagist mode would require only the elimination of the abstract emotional terms: *forsaken, loneliness.*

The impulse to get rid of such abstractions and to replace them with a comparative formula, extended, in the case of some of Pound's poems in the imagist mode, to the elimination of the comparative term itself, except, perhaps, by implication. In his "Ts'ai Chi'h," for instance, the observation half of the formula seems to be all that is rendered:

> The petals fall in the fountain,
> the orange-coloured rose-leaves,
> Their ochre clings to the stone.

Not surprisingly, the effect is much the same, for the observation itself is figurative, and in our attempt to account for the personification "clings" we are made to feel the speaker's awe at the tenacity of the reflected color. More frequently, in such poems, Pound employs the comparative term, as in "Fan-Piece, for Her Imperial Lord":

> O fan of white silk,
> clear as frost on the grass-blade,
> You also are laid aside.

In this poem the emotion is further specified because there is "comment" as well as "presentation," the last line telling us what no juxtaposition of descriptions could: that in addition to awe, the speaker finds significance. It is a comparison in which the imagistic moment of meditative excitement provides an opportunity for an assertion, in this case an assertion about mutability.[27]

Although avoiding assertion is a defining characteristic of imagist theory, most imagist verse does not manage to do it. The way in which assertion is brought into the poems, however, is not usually by means of sententious statement. Howard Nemerov has argued that the failure of imagism is in part because "ideas are not contained in the mere names of things, or even in the description of things, and have to be supplied from elsewhere." This implies, of course, that ideas are something that poetry cannot do without. Nemerov cleverly develops the paradox of thinking otherwise: "Modernism in writing is chiefly about . . . *seeing*, seeing as superior to thinking, as opposed to thinking, and something the poet must do instead of thinking if necessary. One notes already the suspicion of a difficulty, that all this affirmation of the eye at the mind's expense is an operation carried out and a decision taken by the mind, not the eye."[28] While imagist theory may have appealed to the superiority of seeing, it is clear from the poetry that the imagists wrote poems because the things they saw were convenient vehicles for the things they thought. Although poems like Pound's "Ts'ai Chi'h" can be found in the imagist canon, the sort of poem represented by his "Fan-Piece" is much more common. Whatever the theory might dictate, the pressure of the poem to be a statement won out, and this allowed for a greater range of purpose than the passive expression of awe.

Despite the stringency with which the use of juxtaposed observations adhered to the technical demands of imagist theory, it was not, then, for a variety of reasons, always adequate, and it was not, in fact, the most frequent way in which comparison functioned in imagist poetry. To achieve a greater range of emotional experience required making the state of the speaker one of the terms of the comparison, which of course also made the presentation more subjective. Although a technical violation of the imagist principle of objectivity, this is the more frequent use of comparison in imagist poetry. It required only the addition of the first-person, as in Aldington's "October." Most of Aldington's series of "Images" are similar in this respect, for example these three poems:

> A rose-yellow moon in a pale sky
> When the sunset is faint vermilion
> In the mist among the tree-boughs,
> Art thou to me.

> The red deer are high on the mountain,
> They are beyond the last pine trees.
> And my desires have run with them.

> The blue smoke leaps
> Like swirling clouds of birds vanishing.
> So my love leaps forth towards you,
> Vanishes and is renewed.

The explicit subject of the comparison in each case is the specific emotion of the speaker. Three different aspects of the speaker's love, each distinguishable, are communicated by citing their likeness to an observation. The first distich of the third poem is an imagistic comparison such as those we have just discussed. But to use such a comparison to get at feelings other than the thrill of observing a particularly vivid perception required additional material. By bringing the speaker into the poem, the imagists thus increased the range of emotions which could be specified by imagistic means. I will cite only a few more examples of this mode.

Amy Lowell's "A Year Passes," uses typical imagist subjects, but combines the comparisons for a specific effect:

> Beyond the porcelain fence of the pleasure-garden,
> I hear the frogs in the blue-green ricefields;
> But the sword-shaped moon
> Has cut my heart in two.

The feeling of divided loyalties, perhaps, is implicit in the first two lines, but in the comparison of the moon to a sword we are given a better understanding of its nature, and are led to believe that there is no pleasure in either the garden or the voices of the frogs. This is a lament, conveying the state of devastation brought on by the very observations that usually produce a more characteristic wonder. This particular emotion does not seem to be communicable through the objective presentation of the observations alone. A similar undercutting, by more subtle means, is present in H. D.'s "Love That I Bear":

> Love that I bear
> within my heart, O speak;
> tell how beneath the serpent-spotted shell,
> the cygnets wait,
> how the soft owl
> opens and flicks with pride,
> eye-lids of great bird-eyes,
> when underneath its breast,
> the owlets shrink and turn.

The underside of this love is a bit frightening; or at least it is safe to say that the details of the cringing owlets and the "serpent-spotted shell," although not directly said to share attributes with the speaker's love, would not occur unless that love is a complex of feelings, not all of which are unequivocally safe and beautiful, as the love is, say, in the first of the three "Images" by Aldington cited above. Another example of the comparison which functions to specify an emotion, but which makes the speaker one of the terms of the comparison, is a poem in John Gould Fletcher's sequence called "Irradiations":

> The trees, like jade elephants,
> Chained, stamp and shake 'neath the gadflies of the
>   breeze;
> The trees lunge and plunge, unruly elephants:
> The clouds are their crimson howdah-canopies,
> The sunlight glints like the golden robes of a Shah.
> Would I were tossed on the wrinkled backs of those trees.

By virtue of the last line we know that the subject of the poem is the desire of the speaker, although it plays no part in the extended simile itself. But because of the way that desire is expressed, "Would I were tossed on the *wrinkled backs* of those *trees*," both parts of the simile are united in that desire. For what is the speaker wishing? Not, obviously, to be sitting in a tree, nor to be riding an elephant. He is expressing a desire which is specified by the qualities which both these things share, and which the extended simile brings out: an energy which strains against its restraints. What our understanding of the trees gains from the comparison is a formal splendor and elegance, an art able to become nature: the elephants which stamp and shake are *jade* elephants. It is for this transcendent quality, as much a quality of the sunlight as of the Shah, that the speaker longs.

The characterizations that I have given to the feelings communicated by these means are vague, to be sure. Those poems which use comparative strategies to evoke complex emotions are no less vague than those which convey merely an awed state of arrested attention. So long as it was the imagists' aim to reproduce a "mood," they were content, as Hulme put it, "that some vague mood shall be communicated." Since the imagists found the emotions which were evoked by the conventional poetry of the Victorians to be both vague and imprecise, they strove at least, as Pound said, to be "wholly precise in representing a vagueness."[29] Emotion might be said to be vague by definition, when judged by the standard of semantic reference, and so the imagists adopted strategies as precise as possible to produce the sensation of a vague feeling. Pound's elimination of the abstract name of the emotion in his imagist translations, and in his original imagist verse, can be considered to be an attempt to be more precise without denying that the subject of emotion is itself a vague one. Another way of being precise about such vaguenesses was to attempt to communicate their degree, or to use the strategy of comparison in such a way that the reader may measure the extent of the speaker's emotion, as well as understand its nature.

The comparison of more and less, then, as much as the comparison of shared attributes, can constitute the "image," and was employed by the imagists for the creation of subtle effects. Consider H. D.'s "Sitalkas":

Thou art come at length
more beautiful
than any cool god
in a chamber under
Lycia's far coast,
than any high god
who touches us not
here in the seeded grass,
aye, than Argestes
scattering the broken leaves.

The beauty of the coming of Sitalkas is compared to the less beau-
tiful comings of three gods in succession, and the progressive in-
tensity of the descriptions of these gods serves to inform us *how*
beautiful the coming of Sitalkas is. This is all the more so because
the beauty of Argestes' coming is understated, the exclamation
"Aye" being sufficient to tell us that it is understood to be the most
beautiful of the three. A similar comparative strategy is made use
of by Amy Lowell in her poem "Fugitive":

Sunlight,
Three marigolds,
And a dusky purple poppy-pod—
Out of these I made a beautiful world,
Will you have them—
Brightness,
Gold,
And a sleep with dreams?
They are brittle pleasures certainly,
But where can you find better?
Roses are not noted for endurance
And only thirty days are June.

The offering of these gifts and the emotion that motivates the of-
fering are understood by comparing them to the illusory "better."
As there is something about those "better" things which detracts
from their beauty, so are these pleasures "brittle." The world that
is offered by the speaker is cast in a somewhat ironic light, there-
fore, especially in relation to the title of the poem, as if in a world

of illusory "betters" there is no "best." A similar comparative strategy is put to unironic use in Lowell's "Venus Transiens":

> Tell me,
> Was Venus more beautiful,
> Than you are,
> When she topped
> The crinkled waves,
> Drifting shoreward
> On her plaited shell.
> Was Botticelli's vision
> Fairer than mine;
> And were the painted rosebuds
> He tossed his lady,
> Of better worth
> Than the words I blow about you
> To cover your too great loveliness
> As with a gauze
> Of misted silver?
> For me,
> You stand poised
> In the blue and buoyant air,
> Cinctured by bright winds,
> Treading the sunlight,
> And the waves which precede you
> Ripple and stir
> The sands at my feet.

The comparison between Botticelli's Venus and the subject of the poem is introduced as a theoretical speculation, in a series of questions of degree: who is more beautiful? The question is answered when the comparison is created by means of the metaphor in the second part of the poem—no longer speculative—but not in the manner in which one expects it to be answered. Venus was not more beautiful, nor less, as we learn from the final comparison in which the speaker magically becomes part of the painting: she was the same. The illusion of an equation rather than a comparison is created by the fact that we expected a comparison of a certain kind but are actually presented with an identification through the metaphor. "Is like" becomes "is" in this poem in a manner decidedly in the interests of imagist ends. But in order to make this transformation, the convention of comparison has to be exploited for the kinds of expectations it is able to establish.

When the function of comparisons in imagist poems is to measure the degree of an emotion, rather than to specify what it is, it happens that the emotion is nearly always named abstractly, despite, once again, the proscriptions of the theory. The following passages from Skipwith Cannell's "Nocturnes" illustrate:

> v
> I am weary with love, and thy lips
> Are night-born poppies.
> Give me therefore thy lips
> That I may know sleep.
>
> vi
> I am weary with longing,
> I am faint with love;
> For upon my head has the moonlight
> Fallen
> As a sword.

The passages describe a state of "weariness with love." They differ in describing a different degree of that emotion. In the first case, the weariness is overwhelming, but it is able to seek relief, paradoxically, by immersion in its own cause. In the second case, the weariness is more devastating, since there is no hint of any source of relief, and the comparison of the moon to a headsman's sword, like Lowell's use of the same figure, makes the weariness provoked by this longing somehow fatal. Richard Aldington's "Au Vieux Jardin" compares the intensity of two states of happiness, abstractly named, through an imagistic comparison of two scenes:

> I have sat here happy in the gardens,
> Watching the still pool and the reeds
> And the dark clouds
> Which the wind of the upper air
> Tore like the green leafy boughs
> Of the diverse-hued trees of late summer;

> But though I greatly delight
> In these and the water lilies,
> That which sets me nighest to weeping
> Is the rose and white colour of the smooth flag-stones,
> And the pale yellow grasses
> Among them.

The two states of emotion finally serve as the vehicle for the comparison of the respective beauties of the two settings, the beauty of the flag-stones emerging as the foregrounded material. Yet it is ambiguous: is it the poet's state or the beauty of the scene that is the ultimate subject of these interwoven comparisons? It is both, for the two, as presented in this poem, are so interrelated that the figure/ground relationship for which we search is obscured. Comparisons of degree, then, can achieve the same sort of distancing effect, making the emotional state of the speaker a result of the reader's attempt to account for the choice of comparative terms, as noted earlier in the simple juxtaposition of images. H. D.'s "Sea Rose" functions in this way:

> Rose, harsh rose,
> marred and with stint of petals,
> meagre flower, thin,
> sparse of leaf,
>
> more precious
> than a wet rose,
> single on a stem—
> you are caught in the drift.
>
> Stunted, with small leaf,
> you are flung on the sands,
> you are lifted
> in the crisp sand
> that drives in the wind.
>
> Can the spice-rose
> drip such acrid fragrance
> hardened in a leaf?

The speaker is compelled to compare the preciousness of the sea rose favorably to the wet rose on a stem, and to ask if its fragrance can be matched by the spice rose, presumably, out of a state of wonder at the initial observance. But the wonder is tempered by a degree of uncertainty, given the harshness of the description of the sea rose and the lack of an answer to the final question. It is a meditation on the preciousness of the flower's very poverty of typically praiseworthy characteristics, and the speaker's state is not a simple one by any means. A less ambitious use of the comparison of degree is made by Aldington in another of his "Images":

> I have spent hours this morning
> Seeking in the brook
> For a clear pebble
> To remind me of your eyes.

> And all the sleepless hours of night
> I think of you.

Having been made aware of the nature of the speaker's emotion in the comparison in the first stanza between the elusive pebble and his lover's eyes, we find in the second stanza the measure of its extent. By comparing the hours of wakeful searching to "all the sleepless hours of night," the poet gives us to understand the degree to which the lover's captivation fills him.

A third function which the strategy of comparison can have in imagist poetry is to provide what might be called inductive evidence for the plausibility of emotions otherwise, perhaps, unbelievable. In this case, analogy can provide the "proof" of paradox. Imagist comparisons are often found in association with states of mind which are paradoxical, as is the "weariness with love" in Cannell's poem cited above. Here is a similar case, Aldington's "A Girl":

> You were that clear Sicilian fluting
> That pains our thoughts even now.
> You were the notes
> Of cold fantastic grief
> Some few found beautiful.

A state of mind in which grief, somehow associated with the "you" of the poem, is found beautiful is paradoxical, and yet if a suitable example can be found on which to base a comparison, in this case music, the paradox becomes credible. Another poem which renders such an emotion plausible, by similar means, is F. S. Flint's "Beggar," which saves its "image" for the last line:

> In the gutter
> piping his sadness
> an old man stands,
> bent and shriveled,
> beard draggled,
> eyes dead.
>
> Huddled and mean,
> shivering in threadbare clothes—
> winds beat him
> hunger bites him,
> forlorn, a whistle in his hands,
> piping.
> Hark! the strange quality
> of his sorrowful music,
> wind from an empty belly
> wrought magically
> into the wind,—
>
> > pattern of silver on bronze.

Among the details of an otherwise negative description the poet finds music, a music which is significant of the poet's reaction to the old man's forlorn condition: "wind from an empty belly / wrought magically / into the wind." The final line seems to have the force of an argument, in a conditional mode: *if* silver patterns can appear on bronze, by some paradox of perception, *then* it is possible to have this music emanate from this beggar. The comparison between them, in other words, lies in the paradox central to each. Flint's equally long poem, "The Swan," employs a similar strategy, when, after two stanzas of description of a swan, it concludes:

> Into the dark of the arch the swan floats
> and into the black depth of my sorrow
> it bears the white rose of flame.

The possibility of such an emotion, a "black depth of sorrow" which carries with it a beautiful "white rose of flame," is rendered believable by comparison to the swan entering the darkness.

Pound's "Gentildonna" seems to employ the characteristic closing "image" for this purpose:

> She passed and left no quiver in the veins, who now
> Moving among the trees, and clinging
>   in the air she severed,
> Fanning the grass she walked on then, endures:
> Grey olive leaves beneath a rain-cold sky.

"She" caused "no quiver in the veins" when she "passed"—and there is good reason in this poem to take the word as a pun and to understand it to mean when she died—but "now" she does somewhat more than that, she astounds by her ghostly presence *in* the air she once merely walked *through*. The mystery of her enduring presence, whether as a memory or as an apparition, is rendered credible, it seems, by comparison to the perception of the olive leaves, whose color seems at once to stand out from the "rain-cold sky" and yet is not out of place in it. A more straightforward comparison in a conditional mode is H. D.'s "If You Will Let Me Sing":

> If you will let me sing,
> that God will be
> gracious to each of us,
> who found his own wild Daphne
> in a tree,
> who set
> on desolate plinth,
> image
> of Hyacinth.

"That God," who is responsible for doing these unexplained things, changing Hyacinth into a flower and planting her on a rocky foundation as he changed Daphne into a tree, might "be gracious" to us, but only *if* "you will let me sing," as if allowing the speaker to sing were equally unexplainable. The state of the speaker is a puzzling one, restrained from singing for some untold reason, but strangely confident that her singing could bring about graciousness from an enigmatic Apollo. It is an ineffable state of mind which might be said to be rendered precisely, nonetheless, in the comparison to the ineffable actions of that god. Two imagistic poems of D. H. Lawrence exhibit somewhat similar qualities. "Nothing to Save" is an epigram that turns on the paradoxical nature of absolutes:

> There is nothing to save, now all is lost,
> but a tiny core of stillness in the heart
> like the eye of a violet.

The poem "proves," in its own way, that after everything is lost something remains: stillness. The violet is used to compare the paradox to a perceptual experience, that the violet yields a surprise on close inspection. Lawrence's "Brooding Grief" is a more complicated example of the function of comparison as a sort of proof, making similar use of the ambiguous possibilities of perception:

> A yellow leaf from the darkness
> Hops like a frog before me—
> —Why should I start and stand still?
> I was watching the woman that bore me
> Stretched in the brindled darkness
> Of the sick-room, rigid with will
> To die—
> And the quick leaf tore me
> Back to this rainy swill
> Of leaves and lamps and traffic mingled before me.

In this case, however, the paradox is not the mixture of opposite emotions. It is the mixture of imagination and reality. The poem tells us what it feels like to be so preoccupied with an intensely emotional memory that one can be brought suddenly back to an alien reality by the momentary intrusion of an unexpected occurrence. In the last three lines we learn how manifest and how disorienting that reality is.

Comparisons in imagist poetry range, therefore, from an association so similar as to give us unambiguous information, to an association so distant as to give evidence of paradox. They range, that is, from the function of simple analogy to the function of the most challenging of metaphors, the oxymoron. The comparison in another one of Aldington's "Images" is so unambiguous that the specific shared qualities are limited to those named by the poet:

> The flower which the wind has shaken
> Is soon filled again with rain:
> So does my heart fill slowly with misgiving
> Until you return.

This analogy functions to give specific information, and the reader's response is controlled by the limited range of shared attributes. But the comparison in William Carlos Williams' "Fire Spirit," because it turns on an oxymoron, is rich in possibilities:

> I am old.
> You warm yourselves at these fires?
> In the center of these flames
> I sit, my teeth chatter!
> Where shall I turn for comfort?

The feeling of old age, though it is more vague because of the lack of specific attributes, yet is more intense because of the greater sense of disparity which the figure presents to the reader and the greater distance the reader has to travel to discover shared experience. The three uses of comparison in imagism are susceptible to infinite variation, but they all depend on the reader's expectation of design. In the context of many poems which use a similar strategy the expectations become more conventional, and these expectations are available for creating more subtle effects.

In dealing with the image as a figure of comparison we have read mostly short imagist poems, which contain, usually, single comparisons. It remains to discuss the function of comparison in the longer poems which are more complex. Pound included this note in a discussion of the image: "I am often asked whether there can be a long imagiste or vorticist poem. The Japanese, who evolved the hokku, evolved also the Noh plays. In the best 'Noh' the whole play may consist of one image. I mean it is gathered

about one image." Such applications of the term "image" to in-
clude the whole of a long work, especially in dramatic or narrative
form, seem to be at odds with the concept of the image as in-
stantaneous presentation. Hulme contended that to apply the dis-
coveries of the imagists to epic or heroic poetry is a misconcep-
tion,[30] and by implication he ruled out the possibility of a long
imagist poem. In the terms in which we have been discussing the
function of comparison, the extension of one image into a long
work would constitute allegory, and this, as a rule, is not how the
longer imagist poems are put together. But they are "gathered
about" comparative figures.

Thus, we find many comparisons within longer works func-
tioning as they do in shorter works, to specify, to measure, and to
argue, in the context of other strategies. To see what Pound may
be getting at by describing the whole of a long work as gathered
about a single image, it is necessary to broaden the discussion to
include the means used by the imagists to manipulate structural
progression.

Chapter Four

STRUCTURES

Not all objects are equal. The vice
of imagism was that it did not rec-
ognize this.
—Wallace Stevens

Rhetorical Structure

We have seen that the imagists limited their choice of verbal fig-
ures to those that indirectly or directly compare; given the ends
prescribed by the theory, they used comparison in particular
ways. They also limited their choice of available modes of struc-
tural progression to meet theoretical demands.

The concept of poetic structure employed in this chapter emer-
ges from the same considerations which caused me to speak of fig-
urative language as a matter of function: that is, of the ways in
which the reader is made to respond cognitively to relationships
among semantic categories. The basis of structure, then, goes
back to the premise stated by Kenneth Burke, that poetic con-
ventions are those aspects of poetry which "exercise formal poten-
tialities of the reader. They enable the mind to follow processes
which are amenable to it." In an early work, *Counter-Statement*,
Burke is interested in poetic form as it pertains to the psychology
of the audience. Thus, he says, "form is the creation of an appetite
in the mind of the auditor, and the adequate satisfying of that ap-
petite." He goes on to state that certain types of form exist as po-
tentialities within the reader because they have been experienced
apart from the exclusive experience of the work of literature at
hand. Thus, poetic forms exist on the level of literary compe-
tence, to be "individuated," to use Burke's term, in a particular lit-
erary performance. In the last chapter, I looked at examples of

what Burke would call "incidental form," the comparative figures that constitute the convention of the "image." In this one, I will be concerned with the strategies of arrangement which govern the relationship between the larger, meaningful parts of a poem and the whole. (Of course, when the large units of meaning are the two parts of a comparison, as in many short imagist poems, then there is no difference between the "texture" of the poem and its "structure," in this sense.) In his "Lexicon Rhetoricae," Burke goes on to define the types of major forms as the various ways in which one part of a work "leads the reader to anticipate another part, to be gratified by the sequence."[1] As they stand, however, the types of forms he categorizes are confusing. This is because he treats under the same heading both those structures of response resulting from the physical characteristics of words and those resulting from the semantic properties of words. This means, for example, that Burke's "conventional form," can refer indiscriminately to the expectations which a reader has of the prosody of a sonnet and those which a reader has of the development of a narrative. In the first place, the conventional expectations derive from the physical properties of the words (stress or rhyme) irrespective of their meaning, and in the second case they derive from meaning alone.

This confusion has been corrected, it seems to me, in a second major study of poetic structure, Barbara Herrnstein Smith's *Poetic Closure*, which, nevertheless, depends on the relationship between the structure of a work and the psychology of the reader argued by Burke. Smith also proposes categories which distinguish major modes of structural progression, but she subordinates these to a more basic distinction between "thematic structure" and "formal structure" which is lacking in Burke's typology. In defining the structure of a poem as "the principles by which it is generated or according to which one element follows another,"[2] Smith is able to distinguish elements which are semantically neutral from those which are semantically bound. A "principle of organization," as she demonstrates, may be responsible for the creation of expectations of two sorts: they may be "formal," as in the case of a rhyme scheme $a\,a$, $b\,b$, c . . . creating the expectation of a line ending c; or they may be "thematic," as in the case of an "if . . ." clause creating the expectation of a "then . . . ." In the first case the expectation is independent of meaning; in the second case it is independent of the physical properties of the words.

A consideration of both types of structure must ultimately contribute to the description of the principles by which a poem leads the reader through its experience. I will concentrate on "thematic structure" exclusively, for an obvious reason. Because the imagists wrote mostly free verse, one might easily assume that their poems are not conventionally structured. Even if one might find imagist poems which make use of meter and rhyme, and there are some, it may still be assumed that no structural principle is sufficient to account for the construction of imagist poems as a class. But if one looks, not at the formal patterns of imagist poems, but at their thematic patterns—those modes of progression by which the major units of the poem are related and through which the reader is directed—one finds a predominant structural principle in imagist poetry. This principle is used conventionally in imagist poems, as much as formal structural conventions had characterized the verse the imagists attempted self-consciously to escape. Even though meter and rhyme function to contribute to the reader's experience of individual imagist poems, therefore, it is important to understand that such structures are adopted in each case for special effects.[3] The sort of thematic structure which imagist poems exhibit as a class, however, is adopted in order to meet the central demands of imagist theory.

One prerequisite of our ability to recognize thematic patterns of organization (which I have already made use of in analyzing the syntax of comparison in the last chapter) is the assumption that poetry is a species of discourse, something which must be read, and therefore a temporal process, a sequence of events which happens to the hearer or reader. "Available modes of structural progression," therefore, refers to different ways of organizing a reader's experience of the verbal events of a poem as they unfold. One way of acknowledging that the language of poetry derives its power from its ability to *do* as well as to *mean*, is to consider the arrangement of its parts as a strategic means of affecting what happens to the reader coincidentally with their verbalization. These modes are "available" because they are not unique to poetry. They are ways of organizing a reader's experience which are shared by discourse in general.[4]

T. E. Hulme argued for a distinction between two types of poetry. "The difference between the two," he said, "is, roughly, this: that while one arrests your mind all the time with a picture, the other allows the mind to run along with the least possible effort to a conclusion." Imagism, as we have seen, was intended to be the first type, as distinguished from previous poetries. The "image" had to *arrest* the reader's mind, and not allow it to "run along . . . to a conclusion." This is another instance of how the theoretical point of view of the poet cannot be turned to account for the reader's experience of the poem. Inevitably, since imagist poems have beginnings and endings, the mind of the reader is directed through a process, and led to a conclusion. As Barbara Herrnstein Smith says, "what we respond to is not primarily the static spatial array of marks on a page, but the very process of our own performance. It is the experience of this process which is organized by the structure of the poem, and it is that experience which is concluded at the end of it."[5]

Such a condition renders the imagist end of instantaneous comprehension literally unattainable. But, as in the case of the "image" in which comparison can be manipulated to create an illusion of identity by shifting relations between figure and ground, so in the case of structure: the temporal activity of reading may be manipulated in such a way as to give the reader the illusion of instantaneity. What we seek, then, are the ways in which structure may be used to give the reader the illusion of "no process." The imagists chose structures which allowed them to convince the reader that the mind is "arrested with a picture" by manipulating the *way* in which the reader's experience "runs along to a conclusion."

There are degrees to which conventional modes of structural progression depend on the order in which the parts are presented. We would expect those which depend least on some necessary order to be the most capable of giving the reader the sensation that his attention has been "arrested," *as if* by a visual scene. The paradigm for the least "orderly" means of moving from part to part is the list, the simple enumeration of units. Kenneth Burke has called this form of progression "repetitive" because it is "a restatement of the same thing in different ways," the "thing" being the category under which all of the items in the list fall. Under this heading, Burke includes, significantly, "the succession of images." He distinguishes this mode of progression from "syllogistic progression" which would be the opposite extreme, the mode which depends most on the order of the parts, since "given certain things, certain things must follow," and one cannot be led through a given stage until one has passed through a previous one. Smith proposes similar categories, which also reflect the degree of dependence on linear order. She refers to "paratactic structure," on the one hand, in which "the coherence of the poem will not be dependent on the sequential arrangement of its major thematic units." On the other hand, "in non-paratactic structure," she says, "the dislocation or omission of any element will tend to make the sequence as a whole incomprehensible, or will radically change its effect. In paratactic structure, however (where the principle of generation does not cause any one element to 'follow' from another), thematic units can be omitted, added, or exchanged without destroying the coherence or effect of the poem's thematic structure."[6]

I have chosen to use a different terminology to refer to these two major modes of structural progression in order to emphasize certain characteristics of each. Smith's "sequential" and Burke's "syllogistic" progression fall under the category I would like to call *developmental*. Smith's "paratactic" and Burke's "repetitive" structure fall under the category I would like to call *accumulative*. These are not meant to be taken in opposition to the categories of Smith and Burke; I use them to draw attention to the following distinctions.

Developmental structure refers to those modes of organization in which the order of the parts is itself significant, that is, in which the reader is drawn from one part to the next by transitions which involve a sense of necessity, whether by logical, chronological, or causal means. The reader's attention is drawn to the relationship between the parts as much as to the parts themselves and the transition is therefore made on the basis of the reader's understanding of that relationship during the transition. The expectation of continuance and conclusion is therefore a significant aspect of the effect of such a structure, and the effect of the structure as a whole is accounted for by the "end" which makes the structural means which lead to it necessary (*end*, meaning both cause and conclusion, often the same part of a poem's structure). One part of such a structure must be foregrounded, therefore, and any number of parts will provide the background.

Accumulative structure, on the other hand, refers to those modes of organization in which the order of the parts is not itself meaningful, and the reader's attention is therefore drawn to the parts themselves, and to the accumulative effect of the whole, rather than to the effect produced by moving through a sequence of developing relationships. There is no necessary expectation, in accumulative structure, that another part must follow, because there is no sense of necessity holding the parts together. Because the attention is focused on the parts themselves, the reader is conscious that their significance is not a function of the transitions effected between them. There is no proper relation of foreground to background among the parts because each is of equal hierarchical value in relation to the whole. There is, however, an inevitable foregrounding of the whole itself, as the sum of those parts; foreground/background relationships are thus interchangeable. Accumulative structure does not develop; as the rhetoricians put it, it amplifies.[7]

We are at the point now where we may look at how the use of structure enabled the imagists to achieve the effects they desired. These distinctions enable us to understand how the imagists manipulated structure in their longer poems, and to what ends.

Accumulative Structures

It should be evident from what has already been said that of these available modes of structural progression, accumulative structure predominates in imagist poetry. Within this category, the principal means of accumulation is the catalog, illustrated by F. S. Flint's "Trees":

Elm trees
and the leaf the boy in me hated
long ago—
rough and sandy.

Poplars
and their leaves,
tender, smooth to the fingers,
and a secret in their smell
I have forgotten.

Oaks
and forest glades,
heart aching with wonder, fear:
their bitter mast.

Willows
and the scented beetle
we put in our handkerchiefs;
and the roots of one
that spread into a river:
nakedness, water and joy.

Hawthorn,
white and odorous with blossom,
framing the quiet fields,
and swaying flowers and grasses,
and the hum of bees.

Oh, these are the things that are with me now,
in the town;
and I am grateful
for this minute of my manhood.

The trees in this list, with their associations, have an equal emphasis; no one among them is any more important than another, and this lack of subordination between the major units of the poem renders the order of their presentation insignificant. The effect of the poem, then, does not depend on the movement from one part to the next, but instead on the accumulated force of the list as a whole. This force would be unaltered by the rearrangement of any but the last stanza. Similarly, it would only be slightly less if one stanza were left out, and only slightly more if another similar stanza were added. Coherence is achieved by remaining within a category defined by a subject, trees and youthful associations with them. The principle of generation is enumeration.

How does such a structure approach the condition of simultaneity which the imagists desired? The fact that one moves from one part to the next without developing each observation out of the preceding one functions to reduce the sense of process by reducing the sense of necessary movement and expectation. The transitions themselves do not contribute to the reader's understanding of the relation between the stanzas, except in retrospect, and so the particular relation between the parts is not central. Only the relation between *all* the items in the catalog and the final stanza is significant, in the sense of indicating a necessary movement, and the significance of the structure of the previous stanzas is the same *as if* they had been simultaneous. The last stanza explains, in effect, the simultaneity of the catalog by telling the reader that its parts occur together, "now" in "*this* minute" of reflection.

Since the last stanza is a summary, it is also necessarily a development out of the rest. Insofar as it explains the timelessness of the list, the poet has not trusted the effect of simultaneity to come about solely by structural means. But summary itself, as a structural device, aids in this effect by being more than an additional part. It stands for the whole. It functions as the foreground for which the other parts equally provide the background; yet, since it is the whole and the sum of the other parts, this relation of foreground to background is interchangeable. The whole and the parts which it summarizes are substitutes for one another in a way that makes the experience of the last stanza an abstract reexperience of the rest rather than a new experience derived from them. In retrospect, the last stanza organizes the experience of the separate parts into a coherent whole, a whole which is essentially static.[8]

Important aspects of Flint's poem reinforce its accumulative
structure and the effect of minimal process: the use of names
of trees as if they were titles, the parallel syntactic placement in
each stanza of description and sensation, and the use of sentence
fragments, suppressing verbs. But such devices, although they
strengthen the effect by stressing the similarity of the parts, are
not necessary in catalogic structure, nor is the summary statement
at the end. Here, for example, is "Eau-Forte" by the same poet:

> On black bare trees a stale cream moon
> hangs dead, and sours the unborn buds.
>
> Two gaunt old hacks, knees bent, heads low,
> tug, tired and spent, an old horse tram.
>
> Damp smoke, rank mist fill the dark square;
> and round the bend six bullocks come.
>
> A hobbling, dirt-grimed drover guides
> their clattering feet to death and shame.

The principle of arrangement in this poem is also enumeration,
and the transitions which motivate the movement from one part
to the next are therefore not developmental. Only the last stanza
depends on the one before it, grammatically, in the pronoun *their*.
It follows, however, by means of an implied *and*, as do the others.
Aside from the grammatical connection, conveying a unity of set-
ting, the reader is presented with self-contained observations, each
different syntactically and depending minimally on their context.
There is no summary, and hence the effect of coherence is trusted
solely to the structure. Without an explanatory comment as in
"Trees" the foreground is provided by the whole, the unstated
sum of these independent pieces of background.

Thus we might say that the simplest, though not the most fre-
quent, means of creating longer imagist poems is simply to link
short imagist poems end to end, with no transitions to provide the
reader with a sense of necessity compelling a conclusion.[9] Figure
and ground are thus ambiguously arrayed, giving the illusion of
no movement in time. Another of Flint's poems, "Cones," seems
to have been put together in a similar way:

The blue mist of after-rain
fills all the trees;

the sunlight gilds the tops
of the poplar spires, far off,
behind the houses.

Here a branch sways
and there
   a sparrow twitters.

The curtain's hem, rose-embroidered,
flutters, and half reveals
a burnt-red chimney pot.

The quiet in the room
bears patiently
a footfall on the street.

Again, the parts seem independent. There is a principle of arrangement here, however, which gives the parts an order, even though that order does not alter the accumulative effect of the whole. The first three stanzas seem to introduce an arrangement of parts based on hierarchy: each description focuses in on one part of the previous description ("Trees" . . . "poplar" . . . "branch"). At this point the principle of arrangement changes, however, and seems to become proximity rather than hierarchy. We move into the room. A sequence of time is implied, but not necessary: the effect created by the structure would be unaltered by reversing the order of the stanzas. Flint seems to have sought to reduce the reader's sense of process through time by substituting a sense of process through space, as indicated also, perhaps, by his division of the seventh line. Insofar as Pound's definition requires the image to free the reader from both "time limits *and* space limits," such a means of linking separate "images" might be seen as a compromise with theory. But insofar as it succeeds in creating the illusion of observation "in an instant of time," as does the catalog which merely enumerates, it exemplifies how accumulative structure is exploited to reduce the reader's awareness of sequence. In this case the sequence is based on a principle of arrangement which is also not bound by any one part which is foregrounded by the rest; the foreground is the sum of its backgrounds, as in the catalog.

Catalogic structure is most frequently used in imagist poems to amplify one part of a comparison. Here, for example, is Amy Lowell's "Streets":

> As I wandered through the eight hundred and eight
> streets of the city,
> I saw nothing so beautiful
> As the Women of the Green Houses,
> With their girdles of spun gold,
> And their long-sleeved dresses,
> Coloured like the graining of wood.
> As they walk,
> The hems of their outer garments flutter open,
> And the blood-red linings glow like sharp-toothed
> maple leaves
> In Autumn.

The poem contains three comparisons, the first a comparison of degree ("nothing so beautiful as . . .") and the other two explicit comparisons of attributes. Only the first is functioning "imagistically" to render an emotion. The others add information to the qualities of the "Women of the Green Houses," and so these comparisons are themselves part of a catalog of such qualities. Even though the poem is constructed on a comparative model, then, the lengthy amplification of one term in that comparison contributes more to the overall effect than the comparison itself.

No such list of qualities, serving to amplify one term of a comparison, can ever be said to be "complete." For this reason, any poem which depends on such a catalog would not be changed structurally if an additional item were inserted into the list. Catalogic structure has the expansive qualities of an accordian file. For instance, in Lowell's poem, a few more items of clothing, similarly described, between lines 6 and 7 would not affect the reader's sense of its structure. The possibility of such amplification allowed the imagists to compose a "one image poem" of nearly any length. Consider the structure of John Gould Fletcher's "The Unquiet Street":

By day and night this street is not still:
Omnibuses with red tail-lamps,
Taxicabs with shiny eyes,
Rumble, shunning its ugliness.
It is corrugated with wheel-ruts,
It is dented and pockmarked with traffic,
It has no time for sleep.
It heaves its old scarred countenance
Skyward between the buildings
and never says a word.

On rainy days
It dully gleams
Like the cold tarnished scales of a snake:
And over it hang arc-lamps,
Blue-white death-lilies on black stems.

The poem catalogs attributes of the street, employing a significant amount of personification. None of these attributes is of any greater importance than another, but all together are meant to give the impression of the scene. It is not until the line before the last that the reader learns that the street itself is one term in a comparison. With this line we learn that the whole of the description has served to introduce something apart from the street itself: the lamps which hang above it, which become the subject of the imagistic comparison in the last line. The comparison which actually ends the list ("Like the cold tarnished scales of a snake") amplifies one unit in the catalog of the street's qualities. Only the last comparison to the lamps refers to all of those qualities. The function of the personifications comes clear only in this last line, for what hang over the living street are "death-lilies."

If a long catalog serves only to describe one part of a comparison, the poem may be said to have the same quality of simultaneity as a two-line comparison, especially, as in Fletcher's poem, when the comparison comes at the conclusion. It is at the conclusion, that is, that the reader finally accounts for the structure, which has been without a sense of necessary sequence until perceived retrospectively and thus "at once." In the many imagist poems which use accumulative structure in this way, the main comparison may be found at the beginning of the catalog, as in Lowell's poem, but, presumably to better achieve the sense of "no process," it is more frequently found at the end.

Richard Aldington's "London (May, 1915)" [10] is an almost paradigmatic illustration of this mode:

> Glittering leaves
> Dance in a squall;
> Behind them bleak immovable clouds.
>
> A church spire
> Holds up a little brass cock
> To peck at the blue wheat-fields.
>
> Roofs, conical spires, tapering chimneys,
> Livid with sunlight, lace the horizon.
>
> A pear-tree, a broken white pyramid
> In a dingy garden, troubles me
> With ecstasy.
>
> At night, the moon, a pregnant woman,
> Walks cautiously over the slippery heavens.
>
> And I am tormented,
> Obsessed,
> Among all this beauty,
> With a vision of ruins,
> Of walls crumbling into clay.

This catalog of "images," enumerated without dependence on any necessary progression from one part to the next, is made the subject of the comparison in the final stanza. The separate descriptions are brought together in the phrase "all this beauty," and contrasted to the poet's "vision of ruins," so that what were originally perceived as separate parts of an experience are made one part. The fourth stanza especially, because of its explicit comparison to the speaker's state, is an imagistic poem in its own right, similar to other complete poems by Aldington. Rather than reducing the effect of the last stanza, the abstract statement of the poet's emotion in the fourth stanza enhances it, by allowing the reader to associate "ecstasy" with "beauty" and to feel the final paradoxical comparison the more strongly. The word *troubles* in the fourth stanza introduces the paradox which is to become manifest in the end, the meaning of which is thus fully perceived in retrospect.

Among the longer imagist poems of Ezra Pound which function in this way is "The Coming of War: Actaeon," although it structures its successive images with characteristic subtlety.

> An image of Lethe,
>   and the fields
> Full of faint light
>   but golden,
> Gray cliffs,
>   and beneath them
> A sea
> Harsher than granite,
>   unstill, never ceasing;
> High forms
>   with the movement of gods,
> Perilous aspect;
>   And one said:
> "This is Actaeon."
>   Actaeon of golden greaves!
> Over fair meadows,
> Over the cool face of that field,
> Unstill, ever moving
> Hosts of an ancient people,
> The silent cortège.

The last five lines are clearly summary, and the substance of that summary is contained in the final metaphoric comparison of the moving army to a funeral cortège. This is the foreground which organizes the catalog of "images" in the previous lines, retrospectively, into a whole. The parts of that catalog are themselves somewhat ambiguously enumerated, however, sometimes connected by an *and*, and sometimes indicated by indentations in the text, but neither consistently. One reads "Gray cliffs" as a separate part of the catalog, and "and beneath them / A sea / Harsher than granite, / unstill, never ceasing" as another. But the "High forms" of the next line is indefinite: it may be another observation, or it may be an abstraction of one or the other, or both, of the previous parts. The ambiguities of the catalog are used by Pound to give a kind of unity to the list as it is being read, a unity which is nevertheless reinforced in the concluding lines.

The effectiveness of the subtle manipulation of this mode of structural progression is illustrated by H. D.'s "Song."

> You are as gold
> as the half-ripe grain
> that merges to gold again,
> as white as the white rain
> that beats through
> the half-opened flowers
> of the great flower tufts
> thick on the black limbs
> of the Illyrian apple bough.
>
> Can honey distill such fragrance
> as your bright hair—
> for your face is as fair as rain,
> yet as rain that lies clear
> on white honey-comb,
> lends radiance to the white wax,
> so your hair on your brow
> casts light for a shadow.

In the first twelve lines of the poem, four characteristics of the object of this description are catalogued. The first two, comprising lines 1–3 and lines 4–9, are imagistic comparisons, linked by grammatical necessity. The third, lines 10–11, is in the form of a rhetorical question. The fourth, in line 12, is grammatically ambiguous, but also a comparison. It reiterates, and specifies the second, much longer comparison. One might say, therefore, that only three characteristics are described: gold as grain, white (fair) as rain, and fragrant as honey. The concluding five lines, linked to the last comparison as an antithesis, unify these characteristics in an extraordinary last comparison which uses all of these characteristics: as the clear rain that lies on the white honey-comb, so your gold hair illuminates your white skin. What were perceived as separate imagistic comparisons are fused into one. The force of the antithesis is to signal the shift from catalog to conclusion, and to emphasize the paradoxical relation between whole and parts which the concluding comparison makes manifest. The last line is a turn of phrase that requires the most careful contemplation, yielding a description of the effect of this beauty all the more powerfully for its inability to be pictured. If the mind of the reader is *arrested* as if by a picture, it is as a result of the experience of the structure.

Catalogic structure is generated by a principle of continuation, but no principle of closure.[11] Once a catalog is begun, the reader has no reasonable expectation of where it must end. At what point does a list become complete? The comparison so often found at the conclusion of imagistic catalogs functions to achieve the effect of completion by changing the principle which generates the structure and thus supplying a sense of unity which a catalog alone must lack. In Fletcher's "The Unquiet Street," the first comparison, in the third line from the end, prepares the reader for the end by breaking the pattern established in the catalog, as does the antithesis in H. D.'s "Song." On this account, Flint's "Cones" does not have an "ending." The catalog *stops*, but it fails to give the reader a sense of the necessity for doing so. There does not seem to be any means of creating this sense, in catalogic structure, other than by the introduction of some noncatalogic element, as, for instance, the apostrophe "Actaeon of the golden greaves!" in Pound's "The Coming of War." So long as the items in a list are continued on the principle of "this and this and this," because the connection implies no development, the reader is given no expectation of a necessary ending. But with the addition of the final imagistic comparison, the reader is made aware that the catalog is "complete" usually in the sense that one term of the comparison has made way for the other.

Such a closing comparison, of course, may have any of the functions discussed in the previous chapter. In Fletcher's "The Unquiet Street" the comparison functions to specify the emotion. In Skipwith Cannell's "The Dance,"[12] the closing comparison functions to "prove" the paradox of the emotion:

With wide flung arm
With feet clinging to the earth
I will dance.
My breath sobs in my belly
For an old sorrow that has put out the sun;
An old furious sorrow. . . .
I will grin,
I will bare my gums and grin
Like a grey wolf who has come upon a bear.

H. D.'s "Song" ends even more powerfully with such a paradox. In Richard Aldington's "Inarticulate Grief," the catalog is closed by a comparison to an emotion which is abstractly named, and the effect is to allow us to understand the degree of the sorrow being presented:

Let the sea beat its thin torn hands
In anguish against the shore,
Let it moan
Between headland and cliff;
Let the sea shriek out its agony
Across waste sands and marshes,
And clutch great ships,
Tearing them plate from steel plate
In reckless anger;
Let it break the white bulwarks
Of harbour and city;
Let it sob and scream and laugh
In sharp fury,
With white salt tears
Wet on its writhen face;
Ah! let the sea still be mad
And crash in madness among the shaking rocks—
For the sea is the cry of our sorrow.

Only in retrospect do the personifications catalogued turn out to refer to "*our* sorrow." It is only at the end that we learn that the sea is not the subject of the poem, but a comparative term against which a particular feeling can be measured. Having summarized all the parts of the list by abstracting this quality out of them, the comparison allows the reader to feel that the catalog is complete, having a unity which it did not have while the parts were being enumerated.

The reader of Aldington's poem is given another sort of clue that the catalog has come to the end, by means of repetition. In a catalog which is enumerated with parallel syntactic units ("Let . . . Let . . . Let . . ."), the reader may be prepared for the end by varying the expected pattern ("Ah! let . . ."). The apostrophe also contributes to the reader's sense of a complete list. Repetition itself is accumulative in function, but it has more potential than the simple catalog to create the expectation of a pattern, and so can effect strong closure without the introduction of an additional structural element. This is illustrated by H. D.'s longer poem, "Adonis":

> I
> Each of us like you
> has died once,
> each of us like you
> has passed through drift of wood-leaves,
> cracked and bent
> and tortured and unbent
> in the winter frost—
> then burnt into gold points,
> lighted afresh,
> crisp amber, scales of gold-leaf,
> gold turned and re-welded
> in the sun-heat.
>
> Each of us like you
> has died once,
> each of us has crossed an old wood-path
> and found the winter leaves
> so golden in the sun-fire
> that even the wood-flowers
> were dark.
>
> II
> Not the gold on the temple-front
> where you stand,
> is as gold as this,
> not the gold that fastens your sandal,
> nor the gold reft
> through your chiselled locks

is as gold as this last year's leaf,
not all the gold hammered and wrought
and beaten on your lover's face,
brow and bare breast
is as golden as this.
Each of us like you
has died once,
each of us like you
stands apart, like you
fit to be worshipped.

Whereas the structures of the poems which use the catalog exclusively as the generative principle are relatively simple, here we find repetition being added to enumeration to produce a complex pattern. A glance at the ways these repetitions (of words and phrases) are patterned in this poem is revealing:

I
Each of us like you
has died once,
each of us like you
has . . .

gold . . .
gold . . .
gold . . .

Each of us like you
has died once,
each of us has . . .

golden . . .

II
Not the gold . . .
is as gold as this,
not the gold . . .
nor the gold . . .
is as gold as this . . .

Each of us like you
has died once,
each of us like you . . .
like you . . .

The units of repetition are actually two imagistic comparisons. The main comparison, in the first stanza, between "us" and "you" (Adonis), is repeated verbatim in the second stanza. The second "like you" of the first stanza is omitted from this repetition, but it is added to the fourth stanza where the unit is repeated again. The rhythm established by this series of repeated lines is broken by the introduction of small catalogs, and by the repetition of another comparative unit in the third stanza, a repetition begun more subtly by the echo of "gold" and "golden" in the first and second stanzas. But once the pattern is broken by the introduction of a new series of repetitions, the return in the last stanza is able to produce a strong sense of closural necessity—of the poem having come to its conclusion by virtue of having returned again to the beginning. This sense is aided, of course, by the change, in the last line, of the *way* in which "we" are said to be like the god, a rather unexpected conclusion which is the main point of the poem, the foregrounded statement, and which changes our understanding of the praise being given to the god in the earlier lines, its background.

The pattern of repetitions in this poem may be too subtly wrought to give the first reader an understanding of the design, especially since there are other repetitions in the poem which do not contribute to its structural symmetry ("wood-," "winter," "leaves"). Yet they do have the power of accumulation, of focusing the reader's attention on a single point by returning to that point repeatedly. The expectation of a certain kind of likeness, established by these repetitions, is what makes the ending of the poem unexpected. But repetition is also a means of reducing the reader's sense of a developing process, and thus of creating the illusion that the temporal activity of reading is not interfering with the supposed timelessness of the experience of the poem.

F. S. Flint's "Chrysanthemums" resembles H. D.'s poem in some of these respects.

> O golden-red and tall chrysanthemums,
> you are the graceful soul of the china vase
> wherein you stand
> amid your leaves.

O quiet room
you are the symbol of my patient heart.
O flowers of flame, O tall chrysanthemums,
my love who comes

will wave wide ripples of disquiet there,
and a great tide of the eternal sea
will rise at her approach,
and surge to song.

O quiet room, O flame chrysanthemums,
images of my heart and its proud love,
you have no presage of the power that comes
to fill with anguish the essential calm.

O calm wrought face, O sphinx behind the door,
her hand is on the latch.

The repetitions here ease the reader into the poet's state, expecting the arrival of his lover, but serve also to convince the reader that that state is a static one by virtue of its repeated return to flowers and room as objects of perception. He is "patient," as he ruminates about her coming, and the "great tide" that "will rise at her approach" has not risen, so that we feel no sense of immediacy about her arrival. As in H. D.'s "Adonis," it is the repetition that makes us expect a certain sort of ending, and which makes the ending unexpected when it arrives. With the sudden change in the nature of the object perceived, "O sphinx behind the door," the "essential calm" is interrupted, and the reader realizes that the emotion being foregrounded in the poem is not the state of calm expectation at all, but the state of sudden panic (it seems) when the moment comes. What had been thought to be the foreground of the experience, the motionless state of expectancy, is changed suddenly into the background when the "disquiet" that her arrival represents interrupts.

Richard Aldington's "Amalfi" exhibits a similar use of repetition, combined with catalogic structure, but it does not close in a similarly unexpected fashion:

We will come down to you,
O very deep sea,

And drift upon your pale green waves
Like scattered petals.

We will come down to you from the hills,
From the scented lemon-groves,
From the hot sun.
We will come down
O Thalassa,
And drift upon
Your pale green waves
Like petals.

By closing with the repetition, the poet has allowed the reader to remain in the static, ruminating state which is abruptly destroyed at the conclusion of Flint's "Chrysanthemums." The future tense does not get interrupted by the present, as in Flint's poem. The effect of the repetitions is to suggest that there is no movement, except to amplify the same point. The foreground remains the same despite changing backgrounds.

At some point in imagist practice it was inevitable that the desire to create the illusion of instantaneous experience should come in conflict with the desire to record emotional experience, which is not always static. The accumulative structural devices which allowed the imagists to create the illusion that the poem is apprehended in an instant, would not serve the need of rendering emotions which are themselves the result of changes, and which arrange themselves in sequences. "Emotion," said Ezra Pound, "is the organiser of form."[13] The form which suited the imagists in rendering certain kinds of emotion is one that also requires analysis. It is the organization of the poem according to the sequence of the poet's experiences, so that the parts are connected by the presumed association of emotions to each other. Unlike the critic Graham Hough, I do not consider this structural principle to predominate in imagist verse,[14] primarily because any "logic of the emotions," even if different from the logic of ideas, must inevitably be constructed so as to progress developmentally, and the major preoccupation of imagist verse was to achieve the effect of no development.

One result of organizing the poem around the structure of

emotions was a sort of psychological narrative in which the transitions between the parts are presumed to be necessary but are necessarily obscure. An extreme example is Flint's poem "Malady":

I move;
perhaps I have wakened;
this is a bed;
this is a room;
and there is light . . .

Darkness!

Have I performed
the dozen acts or so
that make me the man
men see?

The door opens,
and on the landing—
quiet!
I can see nothing: the pain, the weariness!

Stairs, banisters, a handrail:
all indistinguishable.
One step farther down or up,
and why?

But up is harder. Down!
Down to this white blur;
it gives before me.

Me?

I extend all ways:
I fit into the walls and they pull me.

Light?

Light! I know it is light.
Stillness, and then,
something moves:
green, oh green, dazzling lightning!
And joy! this is my room;
there are my books, there the piano,
there the last bar I wrote,
there the last line,
and oh the sunlight!

A parrot screeches.

It is safe to assert that in this somewhat surrealistic poem the reader is made to supply certain transitions which the poet has left out, by virtue of his stance as a recorder, not an explainer, of feelings. It is assumed that the reader will be able to perceive the connections from one perception to the next, transitions which for the poet are *felt*. By this I mean that such progress of perceptions is only developmental to the one who experiences them as the result of emotional development of some sort. The felt emotions of the poet, presumably, account for the transitions, but the transitions do not give rise to the emotions. This is another example, in other words, of the fallacy of reciprocity. If the reader should supply the necessary transitions, by inventing felt connections of his own, there is, of course, no way to tell if these connections are appropriate, if they are the same connections which caused the poet to arrange the parts as he has done. The reader of such a psychological narrative, therefore, is made to supply an explanation for the transitions, and in this the poet has come to his aid through the title. Flint's "Hallucination," exhibits the same type of structure:

> I know this room,
> and there are corridors:
> the pictures, I have seen before;
> the statues and those gems in cases
> I have wandered by before, —
> stood there silent and lonely
> in a dream of years ago.
>
> I know the dark night is all around me;
> my eyes are closed, and I am half asleep.
> My wife breathes gently at my side.
>
> But once again this old dream is within me,
> and I am on the threshold waiting,
> wondering, pleased and fearful.
> Where do those doors lead,
> what rooms lie beyond them?
>
> I venture. . . .
>
> But my baby moves and tosses
> from side to side,
> and her need calls me to her.

Now I stand awake, unseeing,
in the dark,
and I move towards her cot. . . .
I shall not reach her . . . There is no direction. . . .
I shall walk on. . . .

It is interesting that Flint reserved this mode of progression for poems which record "malady" and "hallucination," indicating, it seems, that the reader could be expected to follow the development better if he knew that the causes of the transitions were inexplicable, except by someone in such a state. The transitions are like those of a dream, therefore, which are only random when we are no longer dreaming but quite logical otherwise. As Kenneth Burke said about the dream, the emotion causes the selection of details, but the selection of details does not cause the emotion. The criteria which Burke established for what he called "qualitative progression," therefore, were as follows: "Such progressions are qualitative rather than syllogistic as they lack the pronounced anticipatory nature of the syllogistic progression. We are prepared less to demand a certain qualitative progression than to recognize its rightness after the event. We are put into a state of mind which another state of mind can appropriately follow."[15] Flint seems to want to put us in such a state of mind through his titles, without which the further states of mind might not follow "appropriately." Richard Aldington's long poem which begins the selections in the first volume of *Some Imagist Poets*, "Childhood," accomplishes the same end: it justifies the arrangement of its parts by informing the reader that the intense memory of psychologically radiant episodes follows such a pattern. One of Ezra Pound's poems from the imagist period in this mode is "A Song of the Degrees." In each case, the apparent randomness of the associations is a means of signifying to the reader that the subconscious follows a logic of its own. The assumption that the reader can share in the sense of the necessity of moving through the sequence of the poem's parts is another sign of the imagist's faith in the underlying unity of emotional and perceptual experience.

Yvor Winters' refusal to share in this faith is a major cause of his skeptical attitude toward such structures, which he, like

Hough, considered to be much more widespread in imagist practice than I do. He used Burke's term "qualitative progression" to discuss the structural method in which "the principle of selection being less definite, the selection of details is presumably less rigid." But when confronted by the effects of imagist verse he found the term inadequate, and added to Burke's typology of forms the category "pseudo-reference," specifically to account for qualitative associations which do not progress according to any principle of selection except that available only to the poet. This ignores, of course, that the principles of accumulative structure, the catalog and repetition, are available to the reader as well as the poet, and are perceived as recognizable structures. Winters' normative use of the term "pseudo-reference" only applies to the extreme use of developmental structures which seem to base their transitions on the assumption that the reader can be made to feel the necessity of movement in the narrative arrangement of perceptions. Winters said that the imagists used such structures because in their descriptive verse the connection between emotion and physical object was assumed but not understood, and he concluded that their poetry was a continuation of transcendental mysticism, but "with half the meaning removed." In a more beneficent mood, elsewhere, Winters said that "many poets have entirely omitted any intellectual sequence from one image to the next, depending upon an emotional unity, and there is nothing to be said against this."[16]

Perhaps, the main distinction between the accumulative structures employed most frequently by the imagists and the developmental structure which imitates the progress of emotions is the difference between outwardly and inwardly directed description. It is reasonable that the imagists would have desired to catalog objects of perception which render the poet's state, given their theory of the object as an "equation" for emotion and their requirement that the poet be objective. It is less reasonable that they should have employed the developmental structure which moves through the poet's experience by means of subjective transitions. Given, however, that the *effect* of such developmental structures is accumulative, because of the difficulty of reconstructing the emotions which motivate the transitions, one has to admit that the difference is minute. It is this impossibility, often, of distinguishing the objective from the subjective in imagist poetry which compels me to discuss this issue in the next chapter.

Chapter Five

ATTITUDES

By the perverted rhetoric of
Rationalism your natural instincts
are suppressed and you are
converted into an agnostic.
—T. E. Hulme

The Paradox of Objectivity

The subjects treated in the previous two chapters, the use of comparative and structural conventions, do not exhaust the ways in which the poetry of the imagists can be characterized as governed by strategic patterns, but I wish now to turn to a strategy which is not reflected in the way a poem is patterned but in the way in which the reader conceives of the poet's attitude toward his subject. I will discuss the reasons which made the imagists want to adopt an objective attitude, although this discussion must give rise, as in the case of the other strategies of imagism, to a critique of these reasons from the perspective of the reader. As I come to analyze more imagist poems in relation to these reasons, I will be concerned with the functions of the imagists' use of an objective speaker, and this will lead, in the last section, to a final justification for seeing in imagism a kind of argumentative theory. The subject of the objective point of view leads to a discussion of argument because it creates questions about the role of the poet in the context of imagism's claim to present the reader with truth, in particular with ethical truth.

Among the prescriptions Ezra Pound gave to the neophyte imagist was to "consider the way of the scientists rather than the way of an advertising agent for a new soap." Put another way, this advice reads: "Consider the definiteness of Dante's presentation, as compared with Milton's rhetoric."[1] As we have seen, the imagists considered that rhetoric resulted from the constraints generated by the poet's commitment to a cause, whereas the imagistic style of presentation resulted from the freedom generated by disinterest in causes. In the manner of the scientist who presents facts without prior commitment to the conclusion which they serve, the imagist was required to present "things as they really are" without comment, or as Pound put it, without "this talk *about* the matter."

From this necessity to be objective follows the canon of imagist rules. "Bad art," said Pound, "is inaccurate art. It is art that makes false reports. . . . By good art I mean art that bears true witness, I mean the art that is most precise."[2] The precision of the image accounted for its ability to communicate *directly*, and the "exact word" could bear "true witness" because it was stated economically and concretely. In reaction against both the didacticism of the Victorians and their over-wrought versification, the imagists sought a form of poetic expression in which the abstracting influence of the poet's ideas was not allowed to interfere with the clarity of the poet's perceptions.

The objectivity sought by the imagists followed, then, from their focus on external objects in order to present reality to the reader without any "veil." As an external point of view, the imagist's objectivity constituted an escape from the self, or an "insertion" of the self into things, as Bergson would say. But, as he had said in *Time and Free Will*, for Bergson this escape was a means of discovering a truer "fundamental self" by casting off a self "refracted" and "broken into pieces."[3] The self, then, was viewed dualistically by Bergson, as either an obscure distortion or as a fundamental whole, and the process of escaping conventional perceptions of reality included the integration of the broken self into a whole. For the poet the attempt to adopt a scientific attitude required a similarly dualistic conception of the self, given that the poet's own feelings and emotions were the ultimate subject of this scientific perspective and external nature provided the vehicle for their expression. In other words, because the subject of imagist poetry was emotions, the scientific neutrality which they demanded was an attempt to escape only the influence of that part of the self which falsified and distorted emotions, and to report accurately the nature of the emotions required the discovery of a real self hidden beneath the surface.

The distinction between the subjective and the objective which the imagists often appealed to, paralleling Hulme's distinction between "manifolds" of perception, was motivated, then, by the belief that the clear vision of external reality, the source of images, was the best means of presenting subjective emotional states. Although Pound defined the "image," therefore, as "an emotional and intellectual complex," he seems to have meant that the emotional could best be discovered and presented by passing through the intellectual, taking *intellectual* to mean the scientific, detached view. We can understand the nature of this "complex" in this way by referring to his comment elsewhere that the imagist poem is that sort in which "one is trying to record the precise instant when a thing outward and objective transforms itself, or darts into a thing inward and subjective."[4] The poetry of the image was an adoption of the outward point of view, therefore, in order that it might faithfully record this instant of transformation to the inward. Imagism was quite clearly a poetry of the self, but of the self through things rather than through concepts. It was meant to deal, in other words, with the way in which the mind subjectifies reality, and it sought to do so by maintaining a strictly objective point of view in the treatment of subjective experience.

Another reason for the imagist's quest for objectivity, which resulted in a similarly paradoxical stance, is illustrated by Remy de Gourmont in a collection of aphorisms called "Dust for Sparrows," which Pound translated for serialization in *The Dial*. "Man," said Gourmont, "is no longer the centre of creation. Yet subjectively he has not yet abandoned that centrality, seeing the universe still exists solely for him, in so far as he is the sole being who transforms sensations into consciousness." Faced with the haunting implication of the Darwinian revolution, that man was not the "centre of creation," the artist could no longer view nature in terms of human values; he could not depend, for instance, on the personification of nature to illuminate the human values in things, as the Romantics had done. The human had to be subordinated to the level of nature. Hulme drew on the theological premise of original sin to argue that the artist must look first to external reality in order not to distort perception through the veil of imperfect vision and he also called, therefore, for the elimination of "anthropomorphism" in matters of thought.[5] Because human perception is naturally faulty, Hulme thought, it must be escaped or purified if the artist is to treat reality faithfully.

Yet, as Gourmont realized, it is the artist who is most responsible for recording the transformation of "sensations into consciousness" and the artist must therefore persist in putting the human first. This process of transformation is what Pound meant by a thing outward transforming itself into a thing inward, and it is the artist's duty to record its occurrence. But this meant that the poet could not consider his own relation to nature as anything but central, it seems, since his concern was with the expression of this occurrence within himself. The imagists were determined to rid poetry of a didactic function, which required the elimination of an overriding moral purpose, such as Milton's, and a commitment instead to a detached view of inward reality. This concern for presenting the nature of subjective reality required the poet to be impersonal only insofar as he did not desire to persuade the reader of an intellectually preconceived doctrine. Imagism opposed subjectivity as a means of setting forth personal beliefs through poetry, but seemed to want to make it a "thing" to be treated by poetry.

The imagists' conception of objectivity stood out in contrast to the highly personal poetry of the Victorians, and it was by means of this contrast that it was most frequently defended. But as we can see from a typical example of such a defense, the very notion of objectivity becomes compromised by the poet's internal subject matter. Amy Lowell defended the "externality" of the new poetry as follows:

> That the poets of the late Victorian epoch were extraordinarily subjective, no one will deny. And this subjectivity led to a refining upon their emotions, until the emotions themselves became somewhat tenuous. . . . Whatever they did they made beautiful, literary backgrounds for a gigantic ego. Each man's ego was swollen to quite

abnormal size, and he was worshipped by his other self, the author. . . .

    Now by "externality" I mean the attitude of being interested in things for themselves and not because of the effect they have upon oneself.

    . . . The "new manner" attempts to put man in his proper place in the picture; that is why it is so at variance with the method of the so called "cosmic" poet.

    . . . "Externality" is the main trend of the "new manner," but of course that does not mean that no poet ever writes subjective verses. He could hardly be universal if he excluded himself.[6]

Perhaps this passage merely illustrates Lowell's own failure to understand the subtle conditions Pound was imposing on externality as a way of treating inward states. But its very literal-mindedness is illuminating, nonetheless, for it reveals the dilemma of translating Pound's subtlety into practice. The further Lowell pursued her case the closer she got to a reconciliation with the subjectivity of the Victorians which she started out to condemn. The real test of a poet's objectivity, it seems, is whether it can be maintained in a purely subjective poem. In Lowell's argument we find both a version of the Bergsonian notion of the divided self (the ego and the author) and the idea that man's "proper place" in the universe is not a central one. These become reasons that the imagist does not write in order to worship the self, but the distinction between this and making the self simply another object to be treated by the poet is obscure. In order to be consistently external, Lowell said, the poet has the obligation to write subjective verses, presumably to make the poem a backdrop for the ego, and to go on "refining the emotions" as the Victorians had done. Her statements finally reveal the inevitable result of the imagists' duality: what they called objectivity, the use of external nature to present emotional states, was subjective. It was not, finally, external, and could only be called "scientific" in a very limited sense of the term. That this has consequences for how we view the distinction between the perception and the idea, between "presentation" and "talk about the matter," is evident.

Pound's conception of the poet as a scientist can be traced primarily to Flaubert's notion of the artist's *impassibilité*, but he also derived it from Ford Madox Ford. Flaubert had said, "The less one feels a thing, the more likely one is to express it as it really is." It does not seem possible to apply this statement to the expression of feeling, but Pound did accept the correlative, that the artist must achieve, as Flaubert also said, "by a pitiless method, the precision of the physical sciences." In the words of Ford, this meant the "rendering of the material facts of life without comment and in exact language." As Pound said in another context, then, the artist must "heave him out of himself" in order to be "simply the great true recorder."[7] Given that the artist includes emotion among the "material facts of life," the question of how he must "heave him out of himself" becomes problematical, for it is difficult to imagine how one goes about dispassionately reporting one's passion, for example. If being a scientist means not being influenced by one's feelings, in other words, as well as not desiring to comment on their preconceived value, then the idea of taking a scientific attitude toward one's feelings must become a contradiction in terms.

Pound's most consistent treatment of this problem at the time, although it does not reduce this contradiction, takes place in his essay "The Serious Artist," in which he was most concerned with explaining the need for maintaining an objective point of view in treating internal subjects. He did so, interestingly, in the larger context of poetry's relation to morals, or "the good of the greatest number." Ethics, Pound's argument runs, requires a knowledge of the nature of man, and since the nature of man is the subject of poetry, poetry provides "the data for ethics."[8] It does so, however, only if the poet conducts himself as the scientist does, without committing himself to the conclusion but simply reporting the nature of man as he is able to discover it within himself. What the poet records is his emotions, but this is not inconsistent with the ends of science, for through the emotions we gain part of our knowledge of man's nature. The facts of emotion must be discovered and recorded by the poet, in other words, without reference to how he values them.

I shall take the discussion of Pound's argument further later on, and deal more fully with its implications in the last section of this chapter. We can begin, at this point, to discuss its validity, as a prelude to describing the poetic effects it gives rise to. From what has already been said about the apparent paradox of the objective perspective, we can see that the distinction between presentation and comment must prove to be impossible to maintain. This is not due solely to the obscurity of the distinction between external perspective and internal subject, but also to the ethical context in which Pound frames his case. In these terms it seems impossible to *present* anything without at the same time implying a *comment* about it, for ethics, by definition, denotes something which is desirable, a purpose which is taken to be worthwhile.[9]

To look at the problem in this way, of course, is once again to adopt the point of view of the reader. However objectively presented, an "image" represents a selection of details. The particular selection must be assumed to have been made for some reason, a reason which is not a function of the subject itself, which is always too large to be contained by a single description, but of the purposes to which the poet puts it. Such a selection, then, exhibits a poet's attitude toward the subject. It is this attitude which makes certain details of a subject relevant while other details are necessarily left out. Given a certain attitude, only some details matter. This is especially the case in imagist poetry which depends on comparison, for to point to a likeness draws attention to special attributes, and it is the drawing of attention that signifies the poet's judgment. Pound's poem "Alba," for instance, might be said to have been composed in the imagist mode of concrete, external presentation:

> As cool as the pale wet leaves of
>   lily-of-the-valley
>   She lay beside me in the dawn.

The poet has drawn attention to certain qualities of the subject, her stillness, her fragile beauty, her rarity perhaps, by means of the comparison. These qualities are not neutral for the reader, and they are necessarily, therefore, assumed not to have been neutral for the poet, since the details chosen by the poet are what have given rise to the reader's sense of value. Feelings, when they are aroused in a poem such as this, are never neutral. One values them for what they are, good feelings, or possibly bad. There is no more doubt that Pound intended praise in "Alba," than that he intended blame in "L'Art, 1910":

> Green arsenic smeared on an egg-white cloth,
> Crushed strawberries! Come, let us feast our eyes.

The reader would be no less certain that this poem intended blame if the ironic comment, "Come, let us feast our eyes," had been omitted, for the selection and disposition of the details are not without purpose, not without some comment of their own. In selecting, therefore, the poet tells us that he has a stance, that he is judging his subject somehow by showing certain parts of it to us. What he is showing is something worthy of praise or blame, and in the showing we are given a reason to believe in this worthiness.

The process of finding and recording "poetic facts," then, is not value free, nor was it meant to be. Pound's assumption in "The Serious Artist," that the discovery of ethical truths is the end of poetic interpretation (since the end of poetic creation is the compilation of ethical data), creates a decidedly moral setting for the poet's activities. Given that the poet is in control of what facts to present, this moral setting leads ultimately to a didactic function, to the presentation of attitudes that are good and in which we are meant to participate. The scientist, after whom Pound modeled his ideal poet, is also, of course, committed to the conception that knowledge is good, and yet we do not call the scientist didactic. We assume that he looks at his facts without reference to his own particular values, and that he is therefore not motivated by a desire to win anyone over to his values. But here we encounter the essential difference between the scientist and Pound's ideal poet, and the reason that the analogy between them must break down. The poet compiles data about emotions, and emotions, unlike the data of the scientist, are relative to value. By this I mean that part of the information about emotions, which is necessarily relevant to their description, is their relation to one's values, to one's sense of right and wrong. One does not feel emotions except that one feels them to be good or bad, desirable or undesirable, adequate or inadequate, etc., feelings which help to make up the totality of the emotions themselves. Such values are persistent qualities of the emotions, and in showing us an emotion in order to make us share it, the poet necessarily shows us the values which give rise to it and asks us to share them also. If the poet were a true scientist, in the sense of keeping utter neutrality about the outcome of his inquiries, and had not therefore discovered his own values yet, because such are the conclusions which the "data for ethics" leads to, then he cannot logically be expected to include *all* the facts about his emotions in his data. He cannot keep his values at bay, he cannot be objective, in his search for this data, because his values are a necessary part of the emotions he describes.

Pound evidently accepted this relation between emotion and value, although it qualifies his earlier position on the poet as scientist, as shown by his statements in 1918: In defining poetry as "emotional synthesis, quite as real, quite as realist as any prose (or intellectual) analysis," he claimed in addition that "most good poetry asserts something to be worthwhile, or damns a contrary; at any rate *asserts emotional values*."[10] Poetry does for an emotion, therefore, what prose does for an idea, *asserts* it. Because the presentation of emotion results in the assertion of emotional *values*, however, Pound's contrast between the advertising agent selling a new soap and the pure scientist does not finally succeed in distinguishing the poet's function from that of the rhetor. Insofar as the scientist is neutral in respect to his own values, and the advertising agent (provided he believes in the superiority of his product) is not, the imagist finally resembles the latter. Pound's negative implication that the rhetor may be a sophist still holds, of course (though I don't think Pound considered Milton to be a sophist), but the implication that the poet has nothing whatever to "sell" does not. To desire to assert emotional values is to be committed to a cause.

Taking the imagists' call for objectivity at face value leads to a way of reading the poetry which overlooks the potential for persuasion that is very much a part of its function. An imagist anthologist has written that "Imagist poetry aimed at complete objectivity, leaving out all rational and moral content, for behind it was a belief that only the image communicates meaning." To such a comment one ought to add that the imagists' "belief" is part of their "rational and moral content," and it is the very fact that the imagists found value in wanting to keep value out of their poetry that renders their quest for "complete objectivity" contradictory. The very factualness of their images represented an ultimate value. Wayne Booth has said that "any statement in defense of the artist's neutrality will reveal commitment; there is always some deeper value in relation to which neutrality is taken to be good."[11] May we not ask, then, what persuasive end is served by the means the poets adopted to attain their objectivity?

The Imagist Ethos

In the case of the requirement that the poet be objective, as in the other problematic aspects of imagist theory that I have discussed, even though the imagists were prevented from attaining the realization of their ends, they were still able to construct means of attaining the illusion that those ends are achieved. What we seek, then, are those conventions by which the imagists created the convincing impression of an objective, scientific speaker.

In the context of Aristotle's *Rhetoric*, the term *ethos* applied to the authority of the speaker and hence to all those means, throughout the discourse, by which the speaker makes himself seem credible. Applying this concept to literary contexts means simply this: behind the literary artifact is a voice, the characteristics of which define the audience's conception of the speaker. These characteristics are manipulable, and thus, from the reader's perspective, the voice assumed to be speaking any work of literature is an "implied author," a fiction. In writing about the implied author in modern poetry, George T. Wright says that "we read into every poem the sounds that we hear, the voice that we assume—as, to be sure, the writer expects us to do. His writing is based on the expectation that we will do so, and on the further expectation that behind every group of words we will sense not only sounds and a voice but a person." He goes on to say that this holds true even though "the speech of literature is different in kind from that of ordinary talk, and the lyric, no less than the drama, is a stylized abstraction of the human dialogue, not an instance of it." That the reader will imagine a person who is capable of speaking any particular poem, even though the poem may not be the realistic imitation of any spoken act, is one of the assumptions a poet uses to achieve particular effects. It is a matter of selecting the characteristics which define the implied speaker, who is, as Wayne Booth has said, recognized by "the sum of his own choices."[12] To the degree that such a speaker is recognized as a "stylized abstraction," by means of the choices that are revealed by what he says, and less, therefore, as a personality, the poem appears to be objective. This "abstracted" ethos is characteristic of imagist poems.

One obvious means by which an objective ethos was created was to concentrate on the external object, as if offering a clinical description. Such descriptions abstract the speaker because they are written as if the description were capable of being made by almost anyone, anyone, that is, with the eyes to see. The focus is on the thing perceived rather than on the perceiver. Amy Lowell's "Circumstance" is a typical example:

> Upon the maple leaves
> The dew shines red,
> But on the lotus blossom
> It has the pale appearance of tears.

Like the morphological description of a botanist, this is offered as if the details were apparent to anyone and the speaker is assumed to be the voice of anyone. Another example, though not as typical, is John Gould Fletcher's "In the Theatre":

> Darkness in the theatre:
> Darkness and a multitude
> Assembled in the darkness.
> These who every day perform
> The unique tragi-comedy
> Of birth and death;

> Now press upon each other,
> Directing the irresistible weight of their thoughts
> > to the stage.
> A great broad shaft of calcium light
> Cleaves, like a stroke of a sword, the darkness:
> And, at the end of it,
> A tiny spot which is the red nose of a comedian
> Marks the goal of the spot-light and the eyes which
> > people the darkness.

The implied speaker of this poem stands apart from the subject of the description, so that the theater audience is described in the third person. "They," the witnesses of the play, are described by one who must be assumed to be present, among those "in the theatre," but who stands apart from them in the attitude of a reporter. This speaker could be any member of the "multitude," should he merely adopt this attitude long enough to consider the scene as something he witnesses rather than as something in which he participates. Again, the situation is typified. This is *any* performance, or nearly so, in *any* theater, and the speaker is a universalized "eye," describing details which are shared by any event of its type.

This mode of description does not eliminate subjectivity, it merely masks it. In each of these poems there is "comment" as well as description. In Lowell's poem, the details are rendered as a comparison, from which the reader is taught something. The shared term *dew* is given new meaning when compared to tears— and since the resemblance is only apparent when the background is the lotus, we learn, by the logic of comparison, that tears lie dormant, seen or unseen according to the "circumstance." We discover then that Lowell is indirectly arguing a "thesis" in this poem, and we do so because it is inevitable that a reader is invited by such a comparative strategy to search for some end, some intention, which is served by the strategy. The "appearance of tears" conveys the speaker's emotional state, part of which is the knowledge that sadness pervades beauty. Fletcher's poem argues somewhat more directly, because the end which is served by the selection of details is a judgment. If we are invited by the terms of Fletcher's comparison to view the audience in the theater in terms of the performer on the stage, then we are led to the conclusion that life is a comical performance, tragic perhaps only because of our ignorance, in the darkness, of the fact. The judgment is already quite explicit in the first stanza.

Because such speakers are abstracted voices, "almost anyone," the conclusions that are reached in such poems have a universal quality. At least one cannot say that the poet has used the poem as a mere occasion for arguing a preconceived prejudice, but has expressed feelings for the sake of their rightness. If the poems ring true it is because the conclusions seem to derive from the observations, and the detachment of the speakers serves to make them more credible.

Pound created such a detached speaker in his poem "The Return," which he once referred to as "an objective reality," calling it "impersonal."[13] But the poem has a voice which, although not identifiable as that of a particular persona, yet nevertheless possesses distinctive human qualities:

> See, they return; ah, see the tentative
> Movements, and the slow feet,
> The trouble in the pace and the uncertain
> Wavering!
>
> See, they return, one, and by one,
> With fear, as half-awakened;
> As if the snow should hesitate
> And murmur in the wind,
>   and half turn back;
> These were the "Wing'd-with-Awe,"
>   Inviolable.
>
> Gods of the wingèd shoe!
> With them the silver hounds,
>   sniffing the trace of air!
>
> Haie! Haie!
>   These were the swift to harry;
> These the keen-scented;
> These were the souls of blood.
>
> Slow on the leash,
>   pallid the leash-men!

This speaker is not personal only because he is not identifiable as a character or even a "type." Yet, here is a speaker who is in the process of reacting personally to the event which he describes. He exclaims, he apostrophizes, he lauds. His ironic contrast between the men as they return from their exploits "with fear" and their reputation (as shown in the epithets apparently applied to them by others) certainly carries judgment. Though the speaker's involvement with his subject is not personal in the sense of reducing the subject to an occasion for arguing some point, neither is it "impersonal" in the sense that the poem is an "objective reality" without appeal to human values and responses.

There may be more or less objective speakers, but there is none about whom we know so little that we can ignore the subjective state which motivates the description. One means by which this motivation is often conveyed in imagism, without personalizing the speaker, is by implying a dramatic situation in which the poem is uttered. Thus, in H. D.'s "Sea Rose," which I have already discussed, although there is no personal reference to the speaker, the form of the utterance directs our attention to dramatic concerns. In addressing the rose as "you," the speaker makes us aware of a dialogic relationship between herself and the subject. Ending in a question, the poem becomes part of some drama, and the circumstances of the drama, both the situation which motivates it and its outcome, form part of the reader's understanding of the poem. Similarly, H. D.'s enigmatic "The Pool," enacts a drama:

> Are you alive?
> I touch you.
> You quiver like a sea-fish.
> I cover you with my net.
> What are you—banded one?

The use of the first person pronoun does not necessarily subjectify the poem if the "I" of the poem is evidently a participant in a drama of two characters. The closing question functions as it does in "Sea Rose," to allow the reader to react with the speaker, and because the poet has withheld any detail which would allow us to identify the creature in the pool, we are made to share the speaker's sense of bewilderment at this strange discovery. We know only what we might see, objectively, but we feel, in addition, the attraction of this rare and mysterious find.

Instances of poems with quite clearly identified dramatic personae may be found throughout the imagist anthologies. I will cite only two examples. H. D.'s "Hermonax" is spoken by a Greek supplicant, a fisherman who offers his strange find to the gods:

> Gods of the sea;
> Ino,
> leaving warm meads
> for the green, grey-green fastnesses
> of the great deeps;
> and Palemon,
> bright seeker of sea-shaft,
> hear me.
>
> Let all whom the sea loveth,
> come to its altar front,
> and I
> who can offer no other sacrifice to thee
> bring this.
>
> Broken by great waves,
> the wavelets flung it here,
> this sea-gliding creature,
> this strange creature like a weed,
> covered with salt foam,
> torn from the hillocks
> of rock.
>
> I, Hermonax,
> caster of nets,
> risking chance,
> plying the sea craft,
> came on it.
>
> Thus to sea god
> cometh gift of sea wrack;
> I, Hermonax, offer it
> to thee, Ino,
> and to Palemon.

The fisherman's gift is similar to the unidentified creature dis-
covered by the speaker of "The Pool," but the poem turns the
event into more than an occasion for wonder. As in other poems
by H. D. (*e.g.* "Priapus" and "Sea Gods"), the persona addresses a
god, describes his own circumstances, and presents an offering.
The values of the fisherman are obvious from his description: He
is a brave laborer who is confident that his humble gift is worthy.
He values the rare above the commonplace, the difficult above the
easy. In creating these values, however, the implied author of the
poem, as distinct from its fictional persona, cannot be said to have
endorsed these same values. The poem is objective, then, insofar
as the character is *shown* to us. Yet why has the poet chosen to
show such a character to us? The reader cannot escape the impres-
sion that something is being celebrated in this poem, if not the
gods whom the fisherman praises, then the relation itself, simple
and adequate, between the character and his deities. To account
for the choice of portraying the speaker in this way, we accept as
the implied poet's judgment that there is something about this
speaker which is worth witnessing. The creation of such a persona
necessarily implies praise or blame, "asserts something to be
worthwhile," as Pound said, "or damns a contrary," just as imagis-
tic description implies the motivation of feelings which are either
desirable or undesirable.

A similar reading is demanded by the way Pound presents the
speaker in his poem "A Girl":

> The tree has entered my hands,
> The sap has ascended my arms,
> The tree has grown in my breast—
> Downward,
> The branches grow out of me, like arms.
>
> Tree you are,
> Moss you are,
> You are violets with wind above them.
> A child—*so* high—you are,
> And all this is folly to the world.

Here, the choice of a dramatic persona is even more clearly the
cause of the reader's identification of the implied poet's attitude,

though that attitude is not a simple one. The poet has chosen to portray a familiar speaker, Daphne, turned into a laurel when pursued by Apollo. In re-creating the moment of metamorphosis from her point of view, Pound asks the reader to compare, and evaluate. That is, because the poet has chosen to give us a new view of a familiar scene, we ask why the choice was made. One reason is the added sympathy which the first person account is able to create. Pathos is aroused by the title, as well, by reminding us of Daphne's youth. As the second stanza changes from first to second person, we are uncertain whether it is the poet speaking or the girl, but our very doubt is the poet's way of allowing us the better to share her feelings, this confusion, this sudden change of identity. Whether the explicit judgment in the last line is attributed to the girl or to a second speaker, however, it is clear that the poet intends us to share in it, and that the details of the poem are accounted for by the conclusion that although "all this is folly to the world," to us (to poet and reader alike) it is meaningful. The poet has not allowed us to infer whether the change is for the better or for the worse, and we do not know therefore whether to lament or to rejoice at the girl's fate, but that there is a paradoxical beauty in the change, and a humbling moral, there is little doubt. Whatever else it may be, the reader is not allowed to conclude that the event is "folly."

It is not surprising to find that one frequently created persona in imagist poems is that of the ideal imagist poet. Such poems reveal experiences which show us what a poet ought to be, and seem to take their place, therefore, beside the arguments of the prose manifestos. In such poems, the implied poet argues for the value of imagistic perception, by portraying a poet who does not argue. One means by which the poet achieves this argumentative balance is to illustrate imagistic principles through translation. Besides selections from the Greek Anthology, they translated poems from the Chinese, such as Pound's "After Ch'u Yuan" found among the original poems in *Des Imagistes*. By this means the poet endorses the value *of* the work if not the values *in* the work, thus remaining "objective," but also commenting on the imagistic qualities of the original which make it worth translating. Especially in the context of the anthologies, therefore, such works advertise the virtues of imagistic technique.

A more frequent use of the persona of the ideal poet, however, is found among the original poems. Hulme's "The Embankment (*The fantasia of a fallen gentleman on a cold, bitter night*)" indicates by its title that it is a dramatic piece. What it dramatizes is the imagist experience of sudden insight from sense perception:

> Once, in finesse of fiddle found I ecstasy,
> In a flash of gold heels on the hard pavement.
> Now I see
> That warmth's the very stuff of poesy.
> Oh, God, make small
> The old star-eaten blanket of the sky,
> That I may fold it round me and in comfort lie.

The poem itself with its alliterations and inversions does not conform to imagist practice, but it is *about* the experience which an imagist poet is supposed to have. Also functioning to advertise the perceptions of the imagist poet are these two similar poems by Richard Aldington:

> *Insouciance*
> In and out of the dreary trenches
> Trudging cheerily under the stars
> I make for myself little poems
> Delicate as a flock of doves.
> They fly away like white-winged doves.

> *Living Sepulchres*
> One frosty night when the guns were still
> I leaned against the trench
> Making for myself little *hokku*
> Of the moon and flowers and of the snow.

The poems deal with emotional states, but they are explicitly presented as states of a poet. They show us the poet's response to war, and argue for the enduring value of the imagistic attitude in such harsh circumstances. Many of the imagists were fond of poems, like these, about writing poems, in which the speaker seems to stand outside the poetic act, objectively describing what a poet feels. In Allen Upward's prose-poem "The Intoxicated Poet," for instance, the poet *of* the poem is similarly distinguished from the poet *in* the poem:

> A poet, having taken the bridle off his tongue, spoke thus: "More fragrant than the heliotrope, which blooms all the year round, better than vermilion letters on tablets of sendal, are thy kisses, thou shy one!"

One wonders why a poem, especially a short imagist poem, must begin "A poet . . . spoke thus." It seems that the reason for writing the whole poem, and not just the quoted poem, is to make the figure of the poet, and imagism itself, the main subject of attention, rather than "thou shy one." The poet *in* the poem has created an imagistic poem; the poet *of* the poem has shown him to us at work.

One aspect of the imagist ethos, in such instances, is the self-consciousness of the poetic act, which itself becomes the ultimate subject. Perhaps this self-consciousness is an inevitable result of imagist theory, in the sense that the poet working in a context of prescriptions must concentrate on those prescriptions as much as on his experience. Many poets are self-conscious in this way about technique, to one degree or another, of course, but it is ironic that this should have occurred in imagism, since one purpose of the prescriptions was to focus the poet's attention exclusively on experience. It seems to have occurred precisely because the theory, or the need to prove the theory in practice, occasionally commanded the greatest share of the imagists' imagination. Even in their poetry they could not escape the desire to carry on the defense of their theory.

At any rate, the objective speaker was a convention used by the imagists to allow the reader to better identify with the emotions, and the conclusions, expressed in their poems. It works along with the conventions of comparison and structure to enable the reader to participate in experiences which are known to be valuable.

Moral Reasoning, Argument, and the Plain Style

I have attempted to support my thesis that the poetry of the imag-ists is rhetorical by applying a conception of rhetoric as discourse addressed to an audience, the techniques of which can be ac-counted for by the controlling intention of affecting that audience in a certain way, and which operate by appealing to shared con-ventions. I have not been able to analyze the poems in this study without occasionally using the word *argument* to describe the effects created by the poet's selection of means. I wish now to in-vestigate the phenomenon of imagist "argumentation" further, and thus to justify a conception of imagism as rhetoric in the more traditional sense of being an art of persuasion. Any system of per-suasion necessarily entails a mode of reasoning and a theory of knowledge. The tradition of Western rhetoric certainly depends on a mode of reasoning based on deductive logic and a theory of knowledge based on dialectic. This Western tradition of logic, however, came under attack by the imagists as a part of their aes-thetic program, just as it was under attack by certain of their con-temporaries in philosophy.[14] I wish to examine the imagists' attack on logic, and to ask what mode of reasoning may have been of-fered in its stead. What system of persuasion, we might then ask, did this alternative mode imply?

To use the word *reasoning* to discuss this process might appear at first to misrepresent the imagist concept of metaphor. If reason must include dialectic, then it would be to use a word which the imagists themselves avoided, since they considered the metaphor to result from an "unlooked-for resemblance" rather than the rule-guided search by which dialectic proceeds. Hulme, after Bergson, defined intuition as the opposite of reasoning because logic is guided by rules, and he therefore frequently decried the tyranny of logic over the mind. Pound also warned of "the tendency of logic to move in a circle," and said that "the syllogism, time and again, loses grip on reality." These sentiments were shared by Remy de Gourmont, who said that "reasoning by means of sen-sorial images is much easier and much more certain than reasoning by ideas."[15] The present problem is to discover what is meant by *reasoning* in such a context and why it was considered to be a more certain means of establishing the truths which the imagists wished to present in their poetry.

"Presenting," or "handing the truth over bodily," as we have seen, was considered to be the means to the end of "direct communication," which happens simultaneously with the expression of the exact analogy between an emotion felt and the "thing" which embodies it. The artist aids the reader in seeing the truth, or, as Hulme put it, "The artist picks out of reality something which we, owing to a certain hardening of our perceptions, have been unable to see ourselves." This necessitated a reformed language, since, as we have also seen, the conventions of ordinary language were blamed for this "hardening of our perceptions." Thus, for Pound, poetic technique required "the trampling down of every convention that impedes or obscures *the determination of the law*, or the precise rendering of the *impulse*." To have thus equated "the rendering of the impulse" with "the determination of the law," Pound indicated that the process by which the imagist discovers the truth is not by means of an arbitrary or whimsical impulse, but one which results from a universal principle of some sort. As a method of discovery, this process is not to be identified with invention in Aristotle's sense, as we have seen in Chapter Two, yet it does follow some law. In the *ABC of Reading*, Pound wrote, "By contrast to the method of abstraction, or of defining things in more and still more general terms, Fenollosa emphasizes the method of science, 'which is the method of poetry', as distinct from that of philosophical discussion." [16] The dialectical method of philosophical inquiry, presumably, is opposed to the scientific concentration on concrete facts, which, as Pound said in 1911, "give one a sudden insight into circumjacent conditions, into their causes, their effects, into sequence *and law*." [17] By applying the principles of this process, determined by law, law is revealed. As we have seen earlier in this chapter, the causes, effects, laws, discovered by this means are ethical truths.

The scientific model satisfied the need for the discovery of these truths, perhaps, but it seems to have stopped short of explaining how the ethical conclusions which follow from the "data for ethics" could be effectively communicated. The efficacy of deductive argument in communicating ethical conclusions is simply that it is able to assume abstract criteria of value from which to argue, criteria which are available to the audience of one who wishes to persuade. The imagist poet, although given a method by which to discover ethical data, was prevented, it seems, from leading the reader to any ethical conclusion by the same method, because that method denies both the persuasive intention and the assumption of abstract criteria. N. Christophe de Nagy has pointed to this problem:

> Pound has to concede that science necessitates generalization, but he refrains from indicating whether and how far the poet or writer is expected to, or rather permitted to, make this generalization himself. It is clear, however, that for Pound this is as a rule not his function; the generalizations have to be made by the recipients of the data that literature supplies, viz. the readers,—who, in turn, will use their knowledge thus gained in non-literary domains like ethics, sociology, or law-making.
>   . . . Pound wants to see poetry free from any moral function whatever that is conditioned by the intention of the poet; poetry, although it provides the data, the "scientific" data, for ethics, does not necessarily have any bearing on man's moral behaviour.[18]

The difficulty is to see how "the data for ethics" can have no bearing on moral behavior. If the reader is to be persuaded of the rightness of the poet's ethics, it must not be because of "any moral function that is conditioned by the intention of the poet." If ethical persuasion is to occur, it must result from the poet's rigorous attempts to avoid being persuasive.

This view of the poetic process must result, it seems, from the imagists' faith that there is only one correct set of moral principles, determined by a natural moral law, which the accurately perceived data of the imagist will point to, just as the scientist's inquiries depend on a certain faith that there is one correct set of physical principles which a correctly applied scientific method will disclose. The imagist poet does not draw conclusions, then, because he need not. Conclusions would be superfluous in a univocal moral universe, because they follow automatically, and the imagist poet was constrained from stating those conclusions to the degree that he was constrained from using any "superfluous word." The poet's task was to find the evidence and to lay it before the reader. Here is Pound on the question of the poet's intention:

> It does not matter whether the author desire the good of the race or acts merely from personal vanity. *The thing is mechanical in action.* In proportion as his work is exact, i.e. true to human consciousness and to the nature of men, as it is exact in *formulation of desire*, so is it durable and so is it "useful"; I mean it maintains . . . the health of thought outside literary circles and in non-literary existence, in general and communal life.
> . . . One "moves" the reader only by clarity. *In depicting the motions of the "human heart"* the durability of the writing depends on the exactitude. It is *the thing that is true and stays true* that keeps fresh for the new reader.[19]

The health of thought, its rightness, could only be maintained by this means if the ethical truth confirmed by the exact depiction of "the motions of the human heart" revealed the inevitable goodness of the human heart. Only a truth which is self-evidently and unequivocally good might succeed in making thought healthy whether the poet intends this result or not, whether he desires the good, or "acts merely from personal vanity," because "the thing is mechanical in action."

To approach the question of how the imagists were able to assume the self-evidency of the ethical good, and what this means to the reader, it is appropriate to recall Pound's statement that the function of literature "is not the coercing or emotionally persuading, or bullying or suppressing people into the acceptance of any one set or any six sets of opinions as opposed to any other one set or half-dozen sets of opinions." It would be easy to understand Pound to mean that the poet's function is not to lead the reader to conviction. This is not his meaning, however. Persuasion, for Pound, was a process that applied exclusively to the communication of "opinions," but opinions could not, in this epistemology, be equated with truth. Conviction, however, was another matter.

In 1917, Pound stated in his essay "Vers Libre," elliptically: "I agree with John Yeats on the relation of beauty to certitude." He did not say what this relation is. Since in the same year Pound was editing the letters of John Yeats for the Cuala Press, the statements to which he was no doubt referring are not difficult to find. "We live in a time," wrote the elder Yeats, when "opinions abound, but not the certitude of belief. Now true poetry, self involved and self absorbed, can only be when there is certitude. I think when we talk of Beauty we generally mean the certitude of belief." Opinions, according to John Yeats, were incompatible with this certitude because "the artist is interested in personality which is infinite, whereas 'opinions are always finite.'" They are finite in the sense that they are shared, but the "self absorbed" poet cares nothing for what is shared. This became, for John Yeats, a test of the true poet. For instance, he said, "Whether James Stephens is a poet or a prose writer turns upon whether or not he is enough self-centred to do his thinking and his feeling all by himself. If he cannot do his best without having someone to assail, or cajole, or persuade, then he is of the prose writers and only incidentally a poet." The intention of persuading anyone of this self-generated certitude is an apparent contradiction, here. If the poet desires to persuade someone, then the thinking and feeling he does is not "self absorbed." "One cannot be eloquent of beauty," John Yeats wrote, "one can only pull away the curtain, and the less said about the vision the better: it would be a 'getting in the way.'" And so, "It is better to be illogical than inhuman; never to be illogical is a poor kind of pride, and belongs to a people who aim at instructing the world, and succeed in being rhetorical and eloquent and always charmingly lucid, yet might do better. . . . Poetry is the last refuge and asylum of the individual of whom oratory is *the enemy*."[20] John Yeats's statements here are at the heart of Pound's antirhetorical stance, his elimination of "opinion" from the poet's province and his substitution of "the thing that is true." Opinion is transitory; certitude endures. Opinion results from being persuaded, *i.e.* coerced into acceptance, whereas certitude arises from the perception of beauty and can only be communicated by "clarity."[21]

    If the end of imagism was to move the reader to certitude, it is useless to contend that it was not ultimately intended to change the reader's mind. The imagists could deny that this process was "persuasion" only because they could distinguish between opinions and certitude, a distinction which is meaningless except insofar as it refers on the one hand to ideas which can be subjected to doubt and on the other to perceptions which are validated by the empirical fact of their existence. The stress on ethics, Pound's conception of the ultimate function of poetry as "the health of thought" or "the good of the greatest number," seems to do damage to this distinction, unless ethical statements are perceptions which can thus be empirically validated, rather than ideas subject to disagreement.

The means by which the imagists conceived of ethics as perceptual data was to equate it with desire. The poetic work, said Pound, must be "exact in formulation of desire." One may not doubt the existence of a desire; it is a datum. If desire always has the good as its object, then one can lead the reader to *ethical* certitude without intending to persuade the reader of any transitory idea. In this way, then, imagism can succeed in changing the reader's mind if it can succeed in making the reader feel certain desires. It solved the epistemological problem of deriving "ought" from "is," in other words, by making desire an ethical imperative: That which undeniably is felt is that which ought to be. Pound could use the phrase "the image of one's desire" as synonymous with "image," indicating that insofar as the reader could be made to feel the image he could be brought to the truth of his desire. Given a certain faith in the goodness of the "human heart," this desire is an ethical fact. Without this faith, the process of imagism could not work. John Yeats also commented in his letters that the reason his son William became a poet was not because he admired other poets but because he "had convictions, convictions that were desires, such as could never be imprisoned in opinions."[22] The mechanism which Pound considered to underlie the communication of ethical truths through facts depended on the same identification of conviction and desire.

Facts of value are substantiated by the empirical fact that they are felt, that they are desired. Since the process of ethical persuasion by means of these feelings entails no logical reasoning, it has no warrant other than the desire to arouse desire, but it needs no other warrant. Imagism as an argumentative mode depends on the clarity of perception itself, which, when confirmed by desire, makes the reasons and the conclusion the same. Pound could call upon art to "bear *true* witness," then, because, like the testimony of the eye witness before a court of law, the evidence and the conclusion are the same, and if one doubts the conclusion it is because one doubts the perceptual faculties of the witness.

Images, then, were meant to be arguments, but of a certain kind. Pound included this statement among his translation of Gourmont's maxims: "Images are not decisive arguments, but, as engravings for a complicated text, they may well serve as a prop or as a guide to intelligence."[23] The arguments presented in imagist poems could only be decisive if a decision were meant to result. No such decision is intended because, although the subject is ethics, the outcome is not proper action. This is left to some other function than poetry. The imagists could afford to be skeptical of opinions because their poetry was not intended to be argument in the sense that it defended propositions. It was intended to be argument, however, in the sense that they considered certitude to be the result of being provoked to adopt a certain perspective. Images are "guides to the intelligence," therefore, because imagism is a method of moral reasoning, an inductive method with feelings of desire as the evidence. The reasons which imagism presented are reasons in the sense of motives, rather than in the sense of premises, but to provide the reader with such reasons was nevertheless its purpose. The sorts of convictions poetry might instill were, by their nature, not "arguable." Those convictions which were the object of imagist persuasion, in other words, were never supposed to have been in doubt. Imagism sought to "change the mind," quite literally, by changing the way in which the mind perceives.

Such a process of persuasion is motivated ultimately by the imagists' faith in the self-evidence of "poetic facts," despite the relativist stance which they often took on philosophical matters. Pound said, "As the poet was, in ages of faith, the founder and emendor of all religions, so in ages of doubt, is he the final agnostic; that which the philosopher presents as truth, the poet presents as that which appears as truth to a certain sort of mind under certain conditions." But such "agnosticism" is not the opposite of belief; it is only the opposite of rationalism. The poet does not mimic the philosopher without the latter's conviction. The poet presents a truth of a different order, the result of a way of seeing rather than the result of a way of thinking. That the two are finally not separable is illustrated by Hulme's attempts to demonstrate why poets "no longer believe in absolute truth," and so must "frankly acknowledge the relative." In his essay entitled "Humanism and the Religious Attitude," Hulme offered the following critique of reason:

> I want to show that certain generally held "principles" are false. But the only method of controversy in any such fundamental matter of dispute is an "abstract" one; a method which deals with the abstract conceptions on which opinions really rest.
>
> You think A is true; I ask why. You reply, that it follows from B. But why is B true? Because it follows from C, and so on. You finally get to some very abstract attitude (h) which you assume to be self-evidently true. This is the central conception from which more detailed opinion about political principles, for example, proceeds. Now, if your opponent reasons correctly, and you are unable to show that he has falsely deduced A from B, then you are driven to the abstract plane of (h), for it is here that the difference between you really has its root. And it is only on this abstract plane that a discussion on any fundamental divergence of opinion can usefully be carried on.
>
> . . . The framework, inside of which we live, is something *we take for granted*, and in ordinary life we are very seldom conscious of (h). We are only led to it by this dialectical questioning. . . . All our "principles" are based on some unconscious "framework" of this kind. . . . We never see (h) for we see all things *through* (h).
>
> In this way these abstract categories, of course, *limit* our thinking; our thought is compelled to move inside certain limits.

Hulme's lengthy critique is finally only an attack on deduction, of course, the alternative to which is a concrete way of knowing which brings one "into direct contact with sense and consciousness." [24]

In his own way, Pound made the same case when he said that "'ideas' as the term is current, are poor two-dimensional stuff, a scant, scratch covering. 'Damn ideas, anyhow.' An idea is only an imperfect induction from fact." Pound did not thereby rule out the possibility of a perfect induction from fact. Indeed, his statement about the imperfection of ideas *is an idea*, one which must be exempt from damnation because a perfect induction from fact. But it is difficult to see how this statement could fail to apply to itself. Similarly, it must be understood that Hulme's more sustained attack on logic does not succeed in frankly acknowledging the relative, for it does not derive from the negative first principle, nothing can be known. In fact, Hulme closed his essay by offering a counter-affirmation, and he did so without attempting to offer any support for it (for to have answered the question "Why?" would have been to expose himself to the dialectical process which he had just condemned):

> But I want to emphasize as clearly as I can that I attach very little value indeed to the *sentiments* attaching themselves to the religious attitude. I hold, quite coldly and intellectually as it were, that the way of thinking about the world and man, the conception of sin, and the categories which ultimately make up the religious attitude, are the *true* categories and the right way of thinking.
> . . . It is not, then, that I put up with the dogma for the sake of the sentiment, but that I may possibly swallow the sentiment for the sake of the dogma.

This is precisely the opposite of what we would expect from a relativist. Hulme never argued that his wholly abstract dogma had come to him by intuition through sense perception. He claimed to believe it "quite . . . intellectually." He advanced his conviction, rather, as a way of explaining *how* the intuitive mode of perception which will reveal those sense data can be brought about. His abstract religious dogma is, in the following paragraph of his essay, used to provide a *deductive* reason for his faith in induction: "The important thing," he said, "is that this attitude is not merely a *contrasted* attitude, which I am interested in, as it were, for the purpose of *symmetry* in historical exposition, but a real attitude, perfectly possible for us today. To see this is a kind of conversion. It radically alters our physical perception; so that the world takes on an entirely different aspect."[25] So, we are asked to convert to this

new way of seeing, which will allow us to see the falseness of ab-
straction and the trueness of things, *because* we hold an abstract
conviction, a self-evident first principle. Hulme's critique of such a
process of reasoning finally applies to his own case. Far from
being a skeptic, Hulme used the fact of the self-evidence of his re-
ligious attitude to question, ultimately, the sorts of truths which
result from conventional modes of perception. Thus, not all ab-
stract categories "limit our thinking," it turns out, so long as the
correct abstract category is adhered to. As a systematic attack on
deduction, imagism ultimately falters because it depends on the
self-evidency of those first principles from which the attack is
deduced.

The imagists' denial of dialectical reasoning in favor of a kind
of argument by demonstration, even though imperfect by logical
standards (and one cannot easily ignore John Yeats's reminder that
"it is better to be illogical than inhuman"), does enable us finally
to account for the imagists' antirhetorical stance. They were op-
posed to rhetoric because they wished the poet's facts to be un-
distorted by his considerations of the reader's predisposition to re-
spond, a luxury which one who is "showing" can afford but one
who is "arguing" cannot—because the disagreement of that au-
dience is never assumed. Even though Hulme claimed that poetry
was necessitated by the fact that "we live separated from one an-
other," that which divides the poet and the reader is not a dif-
ference of opinion but a difference of perception.

In this respect, imagism, at least in its theory, participates in
assumptions about truth and validity which have been cited by re-
cent philosophers as the cause of the decline in interest in rhetoric,
and of the promulgation of various antirhetorical theories. The
concept of rhetoric as an instrument for changing minds is prem-
ised on the condition of disagreement. The fact of disagreement
must be accounted for in any rhetorical theory. When one holds a
strict epistemological faith in the self-evident or perceptually re-
vealed truth, then the fact of disagreement is accounted for, as in
Descartes, by *error*, and it is no longer disagreement in the strict
sense because one or both of any opposing positions is assumed
to be demonstrably wrong. Chaim Perelman and L. Olbrechts-

Tyteca are among those who blame this post-Cartesian assumption for the dissolution of rhetoric into various modern theories of demonstration. The attack on the self-evident, with which their work, *The New Rhetoric*, opens, is meant to apply to antirhetorical theories of logic, but it applies equally to antirhetorical theories of poetic: "Self-evidence is conceived both as a force to which every normal mind must yield and as a sign of the truth of that which imposes itself because it is self-evident. The self-evident would connect the psychological with the logical and allow passage back and forth between these two levels. All proof would be a reduction to the self-evident, and that which is self-evident would have no need of proof." [26] In imagist theory we find just such an attempt to "connect the psychological with the logical"—the conviction that through the perception of things one may attain intellectual understandings of ethical value.

The imagists' particular brand of Kantian "indifference" toward their audience was not motivated by a carelessness of what effect a poem would have on its reader. Rather, it was motivated by the faith that the proper effect is guaranteed, once the reader could be made to see as the poet sees, the faith that if all were given the same means of perception all would see the same truth. The counter-argument to those who deny this truth is not "you *don't* see it," but "you can't *see* it." In poetry this translates into a conception of the audience as either those who don't or those who can't. The imagists sought to minister to the former and directed their polemics against the latter. In criticism this principle translated into a neoclassical principle of good taste. Pound could write, for instance, "You are a fool to aspire to good taste if you haven't naturally got it." He also said, "It is for some such reason that all criticism should be professedly personal criticism. In the end the critic can only say, 'I like it', or 'I am moved', or something of that sort. When he has shown us himself, we are able to understand him." Similarly, he could condemn hostile critics by saying that they ridiculed the "new arts . . . because they do not know what thought is like, and . . . they are familiar only with argument and gibe and opinion." [27] Critics, and other readers of poetry, could thus be easily classified as fools or non-fools, those who get it and those who can't. For Gourmont this touchstone was "sensibility," for Hulme, "intuition." The comparison to Socrates' proof that "the best of these works serves only to remind us of what we already know," provided we are wise, is not a frivolous comparison, considering that in the *Phaedrus* Plato too was making a case for a purified rhetoric, a rhetoric of the truth which preexists and which needs no persuasion. That he was engaged in persuasion, as were the imagists in both their treatises and their poetry, only serves to reiterate the enigma of belief.

The epistemological faith in the self-evident is indeed a necessity in any rhetorical posture such as Pound's when he said that "one moves the reader only by clarity," or that "good writing is writing . . . [in which] the writer says just what he means. He says it with complete clarity and simplicity."[28] Although this epistemology is a necessary condition for such a view of the plain style, the possibility of "complete clarity," it is not sufficient. The plain style of imagism also requires a theory of language in which the relationship of word to thing is ultimate and correspondent, a theory to which I have alluded in Chapter One.

Throughout his writings, Hulme characterized language as an inadequate means of communication, and his reasons should by now be obvious. Because language is communal it limits one to impersonal, stock perceptions. This idea provided Hulme with the need to reform language, to imagine a poetry of images which was composed in spite of language, somehow. He never wholly surrendered the possibility that language can embody "the way things really are." He wrote that "language does not naturally come with meaning. . . . There is *no* inevitable simple style as there ought to be." Because he thought that this inevitable simple style must consist "in the simultaneous presentation to the mind of two different images," he went on to exclaim, "Never, never, never a simple statement. It has no effect. Always must have analogies." (I will deal with the contradiction shortly.) Pound derived his conception of language as an embodiment of reality principally from Flaubert, as N. Christophe de Nagy points out: "What Pound recurrently formulated as the central demand and the safeguard of which he considers to be the function of literature, viz., that 'words' should conform to 'things,' derives from Flaubert's contentions that . . . 'Il n'y a q'un seul mot qui puisse parfaitement et complètement exprimer une chose ou une idée et c'est ce mot qu'il faut trouver, dut-on passer huit jours à la chercher . . . le mot est consubstantiel à l'idée." [29] Another source of Pound's conviction that language could be made to conform to the structure of reality was, of course, Fenollosa, who argued that syntax was the vehicle for bringing language into line with natural phenomena. The ideogram, therefore, was a variety of le mot juste. No matter how Hulme and Pound and Fenollosa differed on how such a language ought to be constructed, all sought to find an ideal poetic language which did not mediate but which conformed absolutely to reality. In each case, the reform of poetry, the purging of those devices which kept language from being true, could not have been carried out without the equal acceptance of two conditions, that language is correspondent with nature and that nature embodies truths which are self-evident once revealed.

This brings us to a final paradox of imagism. Hulme lamented that "there is no inevitable *simple* style as there ought to be," and a few notes later said, "never the *simple* statement." Juxtaposed like this, the two statements highlight the problem of the "simple" style. Is imagism simple or not? On the one hand, Hulme desired a language which by its simplicity allows us to view reality directly, and on the other hand he asked for metaphor to replace the simple discursive statement. This paradox might be resolved by suggesting that by metaphor the imagists did not mean metaphor. The image was not supposed to be a translation of one thing into another or a "turning" of the meanings of words. It was meant to be a literal statement of reality, an ideally scientific language of the emotions. The difference between the poet and the orator, for Pound, was that the poet, like the scientist, "hit the nail on the head." The simple style of imagism was aimed primarily at the elimination of ambiguity.

The plain style of the imagists, then, cannot be distinguished from the high style of the Victorians as the result of a confrontation between poetic and rhetorical modes. Rhetoricians correctly acknowledged the plain style, hitting the nail on the head, to be an available means of persuasion. The sense of decorum, of what means were appropriate given a certain subject and a certain audience, was what determined for the rhetor which of the available styles to choose for a given composition. In the shift from Victorian to imagist poetics, the sense of decorum was redistributed along epistemological lines. On the one hand there was the late nineteenth century's doubt in the abilities of the mind to comprehend reality. On the other there was the renewed faith in the beginning of the twentieth century that the mind, the intuitive, non-rational mind, could grasp and communicate the truth.[30] The former manifested itself in aestheticism and decorative art, while the latter produced, in imagism, an attempt to be clear and precise, and to convert the reader to this way of seeing. To neither of these epistemologies exclusively does rhetoric belong. Each epistemology will find a rhetoric which satisfies it. In the transition from Victorian to "modern poetry" we do not have two poetries, one of which succeeds at taking rhetoric and strangling it and the other of which fails. We have, instead, two rhetorics, each fulfilling the demands of its epistemological assumptions. While we can choose to emphasize how the two rhetorics differ, a more adequate criticism of modern poetry, as I have tried to show, must also account for what they share.

NOTES

Preface
1. Yvor Winters, *In Defense of Reason* (3rd ed.; Chicago, 1947), 21–22; Yvor Winters, *The Uncollected Essays and Reviews of Yvor Winters*, ed. Francis Murphy (Chicago, 1973), 200, 263.
2. Elder Olson, "The Poetic Process," *Critical Inquiry*, II (Autumn, 1975), 74.

Chapter One
1. Ezra Pound, *Gaudier-Brzeska: A Memoir* (New York, 1970), 83.
2. This axiom is contrary to the typical assessment of imagism, and one which the imagists would have disputed, *e.g.* that "the image was not a means to an end: the image was not a part of the poem; it *was* the poem." William Pratt, "Introduction," *The Imagist Poem: Modern Poetry in Miniature* (New York, 1963), 29.
3. T. S. Eliot, quoted by Hugh Kenner, *The Poetry of Ezra Pound* (Norfolk, Conn., 1951), 98.
4. Wallace Stevens, *The Necessary Angel: Essays on Reality and the Imagination* (New York, 1951), 118; Joshua C. Gregory, "Thought and Mental Image, Art and Imitation: A Parallel," *Monist*, XXXI (July, 1921), 426; William Butler Yeats, *Essays and Introductions* (New York: 1961), 215.
5. Among those who have appealed to this remark from Paul Verlaine's *Art Poétique* (1882) are Arthur Symons, *The Symbolist Movement in Literature* (New York, 1958), 46, and William Butler Yeats, "Introduction," *The Oxford Book of Modern Verse*, ed. John Hollander (Oxford, 1968), 87. For a general discussion, see Arthur K. Moore, "Rhetoric's Wrung Neck," *Contestable Concepts of Literary Theory* (Baton Rouge, 1973), 56–72.
6. Stanley K. Coffman, Jr., *Imagism: A Chapter for the History of Modern Poetry* (Norman, 1951), 4–6; see also J. B. Harmer, *Victory in Limbo: Imagism 1908–1917* (London, 1975), 18–24; A. R. Jones, *The Life and Opinions of Thomas Ernest Hulme* (Boston, 1960), 35.
7. The question of whether imagist theory derives more from the originality of

Pound or Hulme is not easily solved, and many who have written on the topic seem to be interested in excluding the possibility of mutual influence in an effort to argue for one or the other as the father of modern English poetry. Thus, Jones in *The Life and Opinions of T. E. Hulme* places Pound among Hulme's disciples. N. Christophe de Nagy reverses the roles in defense of Pound's complete originality. De Nagy is correct in pointing out that many of Pound's ideas were available in the writings of Remy de Gourmont before 1908, but he admits that Pound did not read Gourmont until 1912, well after his association with Hulme, in whose notebooks similar ideas occur. De Nagy underrates the authority that Pound's ideas derive from Hulme's Bergsonianism, even though he admits that it is difficult to determine lines of influence with any certitude. N. Christophe de Nagy, *Ezra Pound's Poetics and Literary Tradition* (Bern, 1966), 71–72. Herbert N. Schneidau defends Pound against the charge of stealing Hulme's ideas, when no such defense is called for and when by his own admission the evidence is circumstantial. Herbert N. Schneidau, *Ezra Pound: The Image and the Real* (Baton Rouge, 1969), 41. Pound himself attempted to put the record straight, unsuccessfully, by saying that "the critical LIGHT during the years immediately pre-war London shone not from Hulme but from Ford." This, however, "detracts not a jot from the honour due Hulme." Ezra Pound, "This Hulme Business," reprinted as an appendix in Kenner, *The Poetry of Ezra Pound*, 307–308. David Perkins asserts that "if we combine the views of Hueffer [*i.e.* Ford] and Hulme, we have the essential doctrines of the new, Imagist poetic Pound was to spread abroad so effectively in 1912 and 1913." David Perkins, *A History of Modern Poetry from the 1890s to the High Modernist Mode* (Cambridge, 1976), 460. Such a dispute hardly seems worth entering, except by those who wish to believe that Pound is the sole authority or who wish to deny him any authority at all. Because the question calls forth such prejudices, and the evidence is slim, it ought to be minimized. The cost of doing so in the present study is to give Pound and Hulme equal authority throughout. The fact is, they agree more than they disagree. The only reason to take Hulme as the "principal" theorist is that his speculations, more so than Pound's, are controlled by an attempt to create a systematic theory of the mind, and Hulme's ideas therefore often function as metaphysical premises for many of Pound's more technical conclusions. Even though Pound may not have derived his conclusions from those premises, they are nonetheless consistent with them. Hulme's ideas may be said to come "first," then, in the logical if not the chronological sense.

8. For discussions of Remy de Gourmont's contributions to imagism, see Nagy, *Ezra Pound's Poetics*, 71–80; and Coffman, *Imagism*, 82ff. On the nature of the Pound / Lowell dispute, which was more personal than aesthetic, see Coffman, *Imagism*, 120–21; Harmer, *Victory in Limbo*, 41ff; and Perkins, *A History of Modern Poetry*, 331–32.

9. Ezra Pound, "Status Rerum," *Poetry: A Magazine of Verse*, I (January, 1913), 125; Coffman, *Imagism*, 113ff; F. S. Flint, "The History of Imagism," *Egoist*, II (May 1, 1915), 70–71; Richard Aldington, "Modern Poetry and the Imagists," *Egoist*, I (June 1, 1914), 203; Jones, *The Life and Opinions of T. E. Hulme*, 35.

10. Glenn Hughes, "Forward," *Imagist Anthology 1930* (New York, 1930), 24. The poets not included are Pound, Cannell, Lowell, and Upward.

11. For discussions of how imagist principles continue to operate in Pound's poetry, after his association with imagism as a movement, see, *e.g.*, Suzanne Juhasz, *Metaphor and the Poetry of Williams, Pound, and Stevens* (Lewisburg, Penn., 1974), 13–39, 75–131; Hugh Kenner, *The Pound Era* (Berkeley, 1971), 360–61, 367, 434; Max Nänny, *Ezra Pound: Poetics for an Electric Age* (Bern, 1973), *passim*; and Walter Sutton, "The Literary Image and the Reader: A Consideration of the Theory of Spatial Form," *Journal of Aesthetics and Art Criticism*, XVI (September, 1957), 114.

12. If T. S. Eliot is correct in saying that "the *point de repère* usually and conveniently taken as the starting point of modern poetry is the group denominated 'imagist' in London about 1910," then one could also look beyond 1917 for ideas about modern poetry that are extensions of imagist theory. T. S. Eliot, *American Literature and the American Language* (St. Louis, 1953), 22.

13. Herbert Read quoted by William E. Baker, *Syntax in English Poetry 1870–1930* (Berkeley, 1967), 118; Ezra Pound, *Literary Essays of Ezra Pound*, ed. T. S. Eliot (New York, 1968), 4–6.

14. Jones, *The Life and Opinions of T. E. Hulme*, 57ff, 126ff. Wallace Martin, "The Sources of the Imagist Aesthetic," *PMLA*, LXXXV (March, 1970), traces Hulme's debt to Ribot and the French tradition of empiricist-associationist psychology. In translating Bergson, Hulme was aided substantially by F. S. Flint, according to Richard Aldington, *Life for Life's Sake: A Book of Reminiscences* (New York, 1941), 169.

15. T. E. Hulme, *Speculations: Essays on Humanism and the Philosophy of Art*, ed. Herbert Read (London, 1924), 121; Henri Bergson, *An Introduction to Metaphysics*, trans. T. E. Hulme (New York, 1912), 7. The vocabulary of "intuition" and "concept" forming "manifolds" and corresponding to "aesthetic" and "analytical" categories, has, of course, a neo-Kantian implication, although it was Bergson's rather than Kant's use of such terms that inspired Hulme. For a discussion of how Kant's distinctions "indicate the direction which poetry might take, in looking for a notable purification," and provide imagism with its scientific ideal, see Kenneth Burke, *Language as Symbolic Action: Essays on Life, Literature, and Method* (Berkeley, 1966), 258–59.

16. Hulme, *Speculations*, 133; Bergson, *Introduction to Metaphysics*, 79–80; Coleridge quoted by I. A. Richards, *Coleridge on Imagination* (Bloomington, 1960), 77. On Hulme's use of *fancy*, see Harmer, *Victory in Limbo*, 107, 176.

17. T. E. Hulme, *Speculations*, 135; *Further Speculations*, ed. Sam Hynes (Lincoln, 1962), 81, 82. Similar theories of metaphor as the original language had been expounded by Nietzsche in his "On Truth and Lie in an Extra-Moral Sense," and by Giambattista Vico, Shelley, and Johann Gottfried von Herder; see Beda Alleman, "Metaphor and Anti-Metaphor," *Interpretation: The Poetry of Meaning*, ed. Stanley Romaine Hopper and David L. Miller (New York, 1967), 105. With Owen Barfield, these concepts are brought back into critical theory: he too considered that the process of making poetic language is to give new meanings to words by creating analogies with familiar words, and that this was the process whereby new meanings came to words in a primitive state of evolution. Thus, for Barfield, the conventional vocabulary of

prose is also a "museum" of dead metaphors. *Poetic Diction: A Study in Meaning* (Rev. ed.; Middletown, 1973), esp. 125.

18. Bergson, *Introduction to Metaphysics*, 16–17.

19. *Ibid.*, 42; Pound, *Literary Essays*, 61, 77; Pound, *Gaudier-Brzeska*, 89; Edmund De Chasca, *John Gould Fletcher and Imagism* (Columbia, 1978), 52; Hulme, *Further Speculations*, 73.

20. Hulme, *Further Speculations*, 84, 82.

21. Pound, *Gaudier-Brzeska*, 86–87. For another version, see "How I Began," in *Ezra Pound: Perspectives*, ed. Noel Stock (Chicago, 1965), 1.

22. Hulme, *Speculations*, 147.

23. Pound, *Literary Essays*, 4.

24. Hulme, *Further Speculations*, 75.

25. Pound, *Literary Essays*, 437, 25; Pound, *Gaudier-Brzeska*, 81, 86; Hulme, *Speculations*, 134; Pound, "The Wisdom of Poetry," *Forum*, XLVII (April, 1912), 498.

26. Robert Langbaum, *The Poetry of Experience: The Dramatic Monologue in Modern Literary Tradition* (New York, 1957), 35.

27. Percy Bysshe Shelley, *A Defence of Poetry*, ed. John E. Jordon (New York, 1965), 25–35. See also, note 21, Chapter Five.

28. Murray Krieger, *The New Apologists for Poetry* (Minneapolis, 1956), 43; Hulme's debt to romanticism is also discussed by Laura Riding, *Contemporaries and Snobs* (New York, 1928), 148–179; Walter Pater, *Selected Writings of Walter Pater*, ed. Harold Bloom (New York, 1974), 60, emphasis added; Coleridge quoted by Langbaum, *The Poetry of Experience*, 43.

29. Pater, *Selected Writings*, 127; William Wordsworth, *Wordsworth: Poetical Works*, ed. Thomas Hutchinson (Rev. ed.; Oxford, 1969), 734; Pound quoted by Nagy, *Ezra Pound's Poetics*, 79.

30. Earl Miner, "Pound, *Haiku*, and the Image," *Hudson Review*, IX (Winter, 1956–57), 572–574.

31. John Gould Fletcher, "The Orient and Contemporary Poetry," *The Asian Legacy and American Life*, ed. Arthur E. Christy (New York, 1945), 150, 148, 151, 161.

32. Ernest Fenollosa, *The Chinese Written Character as a Medium for Poetry*, ed. Ezra Pound (San Francisco, 1969), 24, 21, 13, 8, 22, 23, 7, 9, 10. On the question of syntax, see Donald Davie, *Articulate Energy: An Inquiry into the Syntax of English Poetry* (London, 1955), 33ff.

33. Fenollosa, *The Chinese Written Character*, 28; Pound, *Literary Essays*, 46, 47, emphasis added.

34. Pound, *Literary Essays*, 41, 46.

35. William Butler Yeats quoted by Glenn Hughes, *Imagism and the Imagists: A Study on Modern Poetry* (Palo Alto, 1931), vii.

36. Hulme, *Speculations*, 162–63.

37. A. C. Bradley, "Poetry for Poetry's Sake," *Oxford Lectures on Poetry* (London, 1909), 4–6, 19; Ezra Pound, *The Spirit of Romance* (New York, n.d.), 14; Ford Madox Ford quoted by Clarice de Sainte Marie Dion, "The Idea of 'Pure Poetry' in English Criticism, 1900–1945," (Ph.D. dissertation, The Catholic University of America, 1948), 53.

38. Pater, *Selected Writings*, 130.

39. Ezra Pound, *The Selected Letters of Ezra Pound: 1907–1941*, ed. D. D. Paige (New York, 1971), 18.
40. Richard Ellman, "Introduction" to Symons, *The Symbolist Movement*, xii.
41. Symons, *The Symbolist Movement*, 81; Pound, *Literary Essays*, 5.
42. Symons, *The Symbolist Movement*, 74–75, emphasis added; F. S. Flint, "Contemporary French Poetry," *Poetry Review*, VII (August, 1912), 355, 357.
43. Symons, *The Symbolist Movement*, 71, 37, 48.
44. Hulme, *Further Speculations*, 83, 86; *Speculations*, 166, 132.
45. Hulme, *Further Speculations*, 94; Symons, *The Symbolist Movement*, 66, 63, 29, 20; Ezra Pound, "On Criticism in General," *Criterion*, I (January, 1923), 144.
46. Pound, *Literary Essays*, 21, emphasis added.
47. Pound, "The Wisdom of Poetry," 499; *Literary Essays*, 11.
48. Aldington, *Life for Life's Sake*, 144.
49. Fletcher, "The Orient in Contemporary Poetry," 170–71.
50. Graham Hough, *Image and Experience: Reflections on a Literary Revolution* (Lincoln, Neb., 1960), 68ff.
51. Pound, *Literary Essays*, 55.

Chapter Two

1. Pound, *Literary Essays*, 419; T. S. Eliot, *The Sacred Wood* (London, 1960), 79, 78.
2. Harriet Monroe, "Introduction," *The New Poetry: An Anthology*, ed. Harriet Monroe and Alice Corbin Henderson (New York, 1920), v; Hulme, *Speculations*, 120; Fletcher quoted by De Chasca, *John Gould Fletcher and Imagism*, 162.
3. John Gould Fletcher, *Life Is My Song* (New York, 1937), 59; Pound, *Literary Essays*, 238, 201, 202, 287, 29, emphasis added.
4. Pound, *Gaudier-Brzeska*, 115; F. S. Flint, "Imagisme," *Poetry: A Magazine of Verse*, I (January, 1913), 198. Fletcher gives an account of this editing process in *Life Is My Song*, 71–72; Flint, "Contemporary French Poetry," 359.
5. Richard Aldington, "The Art of Poetry," *Dial*, LXIX (August, 1920), 170; Remy de Gourmont, "Dust for Sparrows," trans. Ezra Pound, *Dial*, LXIX (September, 1920), 223; Herbert Read, *The Tenth Muse* (London, 1957), 122.
6. Pound, *Gaudier-Brzeska*, 83; Pound, *Literary Essays*, 5.
7. Aristotle, *The "Art" of Rhetoric*, trans. J. H. Freese (Cambridge, 1926), 359, 363–65.
8. Pound, in Fenollosa, *The Chinese Written Character*, 23 n.; Pound, *Literary Essays*, 153–54, 283; Amy Lowell, "A Consideration of Modern Poetry," *North American Review*, CCV (January, 1917), 106.
9. Aristotle, *Rhetoric*, 13, 351, 353, 357, 363, 3.
10. Pound, *Literary Essays*, 21, 12, 53–54, emphasis added.
11. Hugh Kenner states the opposite conclusion, saying "Imagism was named for a component of the poem, not a state of the poet, and . . . its three principles establish technical, not psychic criteria." He later goes on, however, to say that "it was English post-Symbolist verse that Pound's Imagism set out to reform, by deleting its self-indulgences, intensifying its virtues, and elevating the glimpse into the vision." *The Pound Era*, 179, 183. While the first two

aims may be technical, what elevates the glimpse into the vision is a way of seeing, a psychic criterion.

12. Pound, *Gaudier-Brzeska*, 117.

13. Remy De Gourmont, *Selected Writings*, ed. and trans. Glenn S. Burne (Ann Arbor, 1966), 118–19; Aldington, "The Art of Poetry," 169; Pound, *Literary Essays*, 9.

14. Pound, *Gaudier-Brzeska*, 87; for Hulme on the architect's curve, see *Speculations*, 132–33, 159–61.

15. Pound in Fenollosa, *The Chinese Written Character*, 7 n; Fenollosa quoted in Lawrence Chisolm, *Fenollosa: The Far East and American Culture* (New Haven, 1963), 168.

16. Gourmont, *Selected Writings*, 125–26; Amy Lowell, "Mr. Fletcher's Verse," *New Republic*, III (May, 15, 1915), 49.

17. It was the determinism of imagism that caused Yvor Winters to call it dangerous, an expressionist escape from the rigors of understanding. See, for example, Winters, *In Defense of Reason*, 50–51, 87.

18. Kenner, *The Poetry of Ezra Pound*, 44; Pound, *Letters*, 23.

19. Pound, *Gaudier-Brzeska*, 88.

20. By "assumed intention," I do not mean a fixed or *a priori* judgment. I mean a construct analogous to Wayne C. Booth's "implied author," defined as "the sum of his own choices." *The Rhetoric of Fiction* (Chicago, 1961), 75. Just as one assumes a purpose for each of the author's choices, one assumes a purpose for all of them taken together. If one's formulation of this purpose cannot be said to be more or less correct as far as the true motives of the biographical writer are concerned, it can be said to be more or less adequate to account for the sum of the author's means. R. S. Crane's discussion of intention is relevant here: While agreeing that the objections to criticism based on intention are unanswerable, he said that "they do not hold, however, when we identify intention with the hypothesized form of a poetic work and then consider how fully what we know of the necessities and possibilities are achieved in the work, on the assumption that, if the work shows any serious concern with art at all, the writer must have wished or been willing to be judged in this way." *The Languages of Criticism and the Structure of Poetry* (Toronto, 1953), 182. When I use *intention* in the present study, then, I mean a hypothetical construct of the end which most adequately accounts for the means, as potential strategies to create controlled effects, which the work employs.

21. H. D. F. Kitto, *Poiesis: Structure and Thought* (Berkeley, 1966), 21.

22. Kenner, *The Pound Era*, 184–85.

23. *Ibid.*, 140.

24. E. D. Hirsch, Jr., *Validity in Interpretation* (New Haven, 1967), 221–23; E. D. Hirsch, Jr., *The Aims of Interpretation* (Chicago, 1976), 3, 87.

25. Pound, *Gaudier-Brzeska*, 78; Hulme, *Further Speculations*, 81.

26. An early, lucid discussion of the problem of periodic revolts against poetic conventions in the Western tradition through imagism is provided by John Livingston Lowes, *Convention and Revolt in Poetry* (London, 1919), esp. 87–115, to which I am indebted for parts of the present argument.

27. Hulme, *Further Speculations*, 91–92; Jonathan Culler, *Structuralist Poetics:*

Structuralism, Linguistics, and the Study of Literature (Ithaca, 1975), 30.

28. Pound, *Gaudier-Brzeska*, 92.

29. Hulme, *Speculations*, 122; Hulme, *Further Speculations*, 93.

30. Pound quoted in Booth, *The Rhetoric of Fiction*, 88.

Chapter Three

1. Hulme, *Further Speculations*, 97; Fletcher, "The Orient in Contemporary Poetry," 167; Ford quoted in T. ·S. Eliot, *Ezra Pound: His Metric and Poetry* (New York, 1917), 26–27.

2. Hulme, *Further Speculations*, 79; Hulme, *Speculations*, 137. Similarly, but less rigidly, Pound said that "in writing poems, the author must use his *image* because he sees it or feels it," *Gaudier-Brzeska*, 86. For a critique of the effect of this assumption on the analysis of poetic "imagery," see Lillian Herlands Hornstein, "Analysis of Imagery: A Critique of Method," *PMLA*, LVII (September, 1942), 638 and *passim*.

3. G. H. Lewes quoted in P. N. Furbank, *Reflections on the Word "Image"* (London, 1970), 31; J. G. Jennings quoted in I. A. Richards, *Practical Criticism: A Study of Literary Judgment* (New York, 1964), 343 n. See Richards' discussion, 343ff.

4. *E.g.* by Josephine Miles, "The Problem of Imagery," *Sewanee Review*, LVIII (Summer, 1950), 522–26; Sutton, "The Literary Image and the Reader," esp. 123; as well as by Furbank, Hornstein, and Richards in the above works.

5. Laurence Perrine, *Sound and Sense: An Introduction to Poetry* (4th ed.; New York, 1973), 49.

6. Hulme, *Further Speculations*, 84, 73, emphasis added. See also Pound, *The Spirit of Romance*, 177.

7. Pound compared his "Metro" poem to a Japanese haiku:

> The footsteps of the cat upon the snow:
> (are like) plum-blossoms.

and commented that "the words 'are like' would not occur in the original, but I add them for clarity," indicating that the comparison was meant to be understood but that Pound saw some advantage in choosing to imply it by leaving out the comparative term. *Gaudier-Brzeska*, 89.

8. Joseph Frank, "Spatial Form in Literature," *Criticism: The Foundations of Modern Literary Judgment*, ed. Mark Schorer, Josephine Miles, and Gordon McKenzie (Rev. ed.; New York, 1958), 383, 383–84.

9. Hugh Witemeyer, *The Poetry of Ezra Pound: Forms and Renewal, 1908–1920* (Berkeley, 1969), 35. See also, Furbank, *Reflections on the Word "Image"*, 42–43.

10. Witemeyer, *The Poetry of Ezra Pound: Forms and Renewal*, 142. Fletcher cites a version of the same poem translated by Arthur Waley which is more modern than Giles's but which ends by specifying the emotion: "Longing for that lovely lady, / How can I bring my aching heart to rest?" "The Orient in Contemporary Poetry," 166.

11. Pound, *Literary Essays*, 5.

12. Donald Davie raises this semantic commonplace in his discussion of imagism, *Articulate Energy*, 96ff, as does Yvor Winters, *In Defense of Reason*, 17.
13. Furbank, *Reflections on the Word "Image"*, 13.
14. *Ibid.*, 72.
15. Ray Frazer, "The Origin of the Term 'Image,'" *English Literary History*, XXVII (June, 1960), 149; Christine Brooke-Rose, *A Grammar of Metaphor* (London, 1958), 13; Hugh Kenner, *The Art of Poetry* (New York, 1959), 37ff. See Furbank, *Reflections on the Word "Image"*, 72ff.
16. J. V. Cunningham, *Tradition and Poetic Structure: Essays in Literary History and Criticism* (Denver, 1960), 46, 45; Miles, "The Problem of Imagery," 523.
17. Davie, *Articulate Energy*, 52; Sutton, "The Literary Image and the Reader," 123.
18. Fenollosa, *The Chinese Written Character*, 26.
19. Davie, *Articulate Energy*, 79, 19; Cunningham, *Tradition and Poetic Structure*, 22.
20. Kenneth Burke, *Counter-Statement* (Chicago, 1957), 50, 48, 142–43, emphasis added.
21. Pound, *Gaudier-Brzeska*, 88, 120–21; "Preface," *Some Imagist Poets 1916: An Annual Anthology* (Boston, 1916), vi.
22. T. S. Eliot, *Selected Essays* (New ed.; New York, 1960), esp. 243, 247–48; Jones, *The Life and Opinions of T. E. Hulme*, 52, emphasis added.
23. Josephine Miles, "Reading Poems," *English Journal*, LII (March, 1963), 158.
24. Davie, *Articulate Energy*, 101–102.
25. Fenollosa, *The Chinese Written Character*, 23.
26. Flint, "The History of Imagism," 70.
27. Hugh Witemeyer cites Herbert Giles's version of this poem also:

> O Fair white silk, fresh from the weaver's loom,
> Clear as frost, bright as the winter's snow—
> See! friendship fashions out of thee a fan,
> Round as the round moon shines in heaven above,
> At home, abroad, a close companion thou,
> Stirring at every move the grateful gale.
> And yet I fear, ah me! that autumn chills
> Cooling the dying summer's torrid rage,
> Will see thee laid neglected on the shelf,
> All thoughts of bygone days, like them bygone.

Witemeyer comments: "The principles of Imagist economy enable Pound to achieve this astonishing condensation, in which nothing essential is omitted from the original." *The Poetry of Ezra Pound: Forms and Renewal*, 143. To make this judgment requires a sense of what is "essential" which derives, after the fact, from the interpretation which Pound's version gives to the poem.
28. Howard Nemerov, *Figures of Thought: Speculations on the Meaning of Poetry and Other Essays* (Boston, 1978), 154, 152.
29. Hulme, *Further Speculations*, 71; Pound, *Literary Essays*, 44.
30. Pound, *Gaudier-Brzeska*, 94 n; Hulme, *Further Speculations*, 72.

Chapter Four

1. Burke, *Counter-Statement*, 31, 46, 124.
2. Barbara Herrnstein Smith, *Poetic Closure: A Study of How Poems End* (Chicago, 1968), 4.
3. See Smith, however, on the formal conventions of free verse, *ibid.*, 84–95.
4. In arguing for a reader-oriented criticism, Stanley Fish also mentions that such a method does not begin with the assumption of literature's uniqueness. While agreeing with the basic impulses of Fish's argument in "Literature and the Reader: Affective Stylistics," I am trusting that my analyses of poems will suffice to demonstrate that I do not hold too literally to all his working assumptions. Fish does suggest that his principles extend to units larger than words, but his analyses have been criticized for their failure to account for other aspects of the reader's experience than "the developing responses of the reader in relation to the words as they succeed each other in time," especially the patterning of those responses which results from the reader's perception of ideas in conventional structural relations. Fish's linear method might be said to undervalue structure, as I am using it here, as a conventional strategy for controlling responses. *Self-Consuming Artifacts: The Experience of Seventeenth Century Literature* (Berkeley, 1972), 408, 399, 387–88.
5. Hulme, *Further Speculations*, 74; Smith, *Poetic Closure*, 10.
6. Burke, *Counter-Statement*, 125, 124; Smith, *Poetic Closure*, 99.
7. Distinctions made by Josephine Miles resemble the types of progression which I have called developmental and accumulative, and her conclusion that modern poetry became "phrasal" at the turn of the century parallels my conclusions in this chapter. "Clausal poems," she writes, "tend to be stanzaic and active poems, working out an argument or narrative in clearly defined stages and formal external order. Phrasal poems, and phrasal eras, on the other hand, emphasize line-by-line progression, and cumulative participial modifications in description and invocation without stress on external rhyming or grouping." *Eras and Modes in English Poetry* (Berkeley, 1964), 11.
8. One might say that the same is true of a conclusion to a series of developing stanzas related logically, *i.e.* that the conclusion organizes the experience of the rest, in retrospect, into a coherent, static whole. The difference, however, would be that this whole would seem to be static only in relation to the conclusion, its unity depending on a clear sense of a beginning, an ending, and steps along the way. The first five stanzas of Flint's poem might be said to resemble the relation of inductive, rather than deductive, parts to a conclusion, the validity of which would depend on the sum of the parts present but not their arrangement. A deductive conclusion can be said to depend on the validity of the relation to the premise immediately "prior." Induction proceeds accumulatively whereas deduction proceeds developmentally, a distinction which is relevant to the kind of "proof" imagist poems offer, as discussed in Chapters Three and Five.
9. Warren Ramsey writes, "Structurally speaking, the Imagist poem tends to be an elaboration of a single visual image, or else it places end to end a series of such images, in a compound but not a complex relation. The ambitious poets

among the Imagists—Pound insofar as he was an Imagist—sensed limitations of method, straitness of viewpoint, within their program, and began to cast about for techniques which would permit them to respond to complex realities in a complex way." The structural method which Ramsey says Pound learned from LaForgue as a substitute for the imagistic compound, "anachronism methodical, the past continuous, and all ages contemporaneous," is, I would contend, but another way of using accumulative structure rather than a substitute for it. "Pound, LaForgue, and Dramatic Structure," *Comparative Literature*, III (Winter, 1951), 48, 55. See also, Baker, *Syntax in English Poetry*, 129–30, 153–54, for discussions of catalogic structure in imagist and earlier poetry.

10. Richard Aldington, "The Imagists," *Bruno Chap Books* (New York, 1915), 75. My structural analysis overlooks Aldington's sexual wordplay, which no doubt indicates more precisely the nature of the emotion conveyed in the final comparison.

11. See Smith, *Poetic Closure*, 2–4, 98ff.

12. Skipwith Cannell, "The Dance," *New Freewoman*, I (September, 1, 1913), 114.

13. Pound quoted in Nagy, *Ezra Pound's Poetics*, 26.

14. Hough, *Image and Experience*, 18ff.

15. Burke, *Counter-Statement*, 125.

16. Winters, *In Defense of Reason*, 58, 47–56; Winters, *Uncollected Essays*, 213.

Chapter Five

1. Pound, *Literary Essays*, 6–7.

2. *Ibid.*, 43–44.

3. Henri Bergson, *Time and Free Will: An Essay on the Immediate Data of Consciousness*, trans. F. L. Pogson (New York, 1960), 128–29, 138–39.

4. Pound, *Gaudier-Brzeska*, 89.

5. Gourmont, "Dust for Sparrows," 368; Hulme, *Speculations*, 45, 47, 64–71.

6. Amy Lowell, "The New Manner in Modern Poetry," *New Republic*, VIII (March 4, 1916), 124–25.

7. On Flaubert, see Nagy, *Ezra Pound's Poetics*, 50ff; Ford quoted in Dion, "The Idea of 'Pure Poetry,'" 53; Pound, *Literary Essays*, 299–300.

8. Pound, *Literary Essays*, 41, 43.

9. See Kenneth Burke, *A Rhetoric of Motives* (Berkeley, 1969), 88–90.

10. Pound, *Literary Essays*, 324 n, emphasis added.

11. Pratt, "Introduction," *The Imagist Poem*, 29–30; Booth, *The Rhetoric of Fiction*, 68.

12. George T. Wright, *The Poet in the Poem: The Personae of Eliot, Yeats, and Pound* (Berkeley, 1962), 6, 21; Booth, *The Rhetoric of Fiction*, 75.

13. Pound, *Gaudier-Brzeska*, 85.

14. For example, John Maynard Keynes candidly described some of the assumptions which motivated the Cambridge philosophers and their Bloomsbury followers before 1914, under the influence of Bertrand Russell and G. E. Moore, in terms which parallel assumptions motivating the imagists during

the same period: "Nothing mattered but states of mind. . . . These states of mind were not associated with action. . . . They consisted of timeless, passionate states of contemplation and communion. . . . How did we know what states of mind were good? This was a matter of direct inspection, of direct unanalysable intuition about which it was useless and impossible to argue. . . . We regarded all this as entirely rational and scientific in character. . . . You could make essentially vague notions clear by using precise language about them . . . safely released from the outward constraints of convention." "My Early Beliefs," *The Collected Writings of John Maynard Keynes* (16 vols.; London, 1972), X, 436, 437, 438, 440, 447. The purified intuitive reason of these philosophers had the same attributes as the purified poetic reason of the imagists, including the antirhetorical bias, and met the same end; Keynes indicates that the outbreak of the world war had a rending effect on these assumptions, as it did on the ideals of the imagist movement. After the war, for both groups, the ideals of objectivity and scientific absolutism lost their appeal. The poets all moved away from imagist technique, to one degree or another.

15. Pound quoted in Nänny, *Ezra Pound: Poetics for an Electric Age*, 50–51; Gourmont, *Selected Writings*, 122.

16. Hulme, *Speculations*, 156; Pound, *Literary Essays*, 9, emphasis added; Ezra Pound, *ABC of Reading* (New York, 1960), 20.

17. Pound quoted in Nänny, *Ezra Pound: Poetics for an Electric Age*, 58, emphasis added.

18. Nagy, *Ezra Pound's Poetics*, 32.

19. Pound, *Literary Essays*, 22, emphasis added.

20. Pound, *ibid.*, 13; John Butler Yeats, *Passages from the Letters of John Butler Yeats: Selected by Ezra Pound* (Churchtown, Dundrum, 1917), 32, 49, 34, 53.

21. Again, we can note the heritage of these ideas in romanticism, especially as they are presented in Shelley's argument that poetry produces "moral improvement" by "lifting the veil from the hidden beauty of the world," but not if the poet gives only "his own conceptions of right and wrong, which are usually of his time and place." For Shelley, also, "poetry is not like reasoning, a power to be exerted according to the determination of the will," and therefore it "is not subject to the controul of the active powers of the mind." It tells the truth, rather, because "it compels us to feel that which we perceive . . . after it has been annihilated in our minds by the recurrence of impressions blunted by reiteration." *A Defence of Poetry*, 39, 40, 41, 70, 76, 75.

22. John Yeats, *Passages from the Letters*, 54.

23. Gourmont, "Dust for Sparrows," 369.

24. Pound, "The Wisdom of Poetry," 499; Hulme, *Further Speculations*, 71; Hulme, *Speculations*, 64–66, 158.

25. Pound, *Literary Essays*, 267; Hulme, *Speculations*, 70–71.

26. Chaim Perelman and L. Olbrechts-Tyteca, *The New Rhetoric: A Treatise on Argumentation*, trans. John Wilkinson and Purcell Weaver (Notre Dame, 1969), 3–4.

27. Pound, *Literary Essays*, 46, 56; Pound, *Gaudier-Brzeska*, 87.

28. Pound, *Literary Essays*, 50.

29. Hulme, *Further Speculations*, 83–84, 87; Nagy, *Ezra Pound's Poetics*, 54.
30. Stanley Fish develops a similar explanation of an epistemological conflict in the seventeenth century and its consequences for our understanding of the "plain style." *Self-Consuming Artifacts*, 377.

BIBLIOGRAPHY

Collections of Imagist Poetry

Hughes, Glenn, and Ford Madox Ford, eds. *Imagist Anthology 1930*. New York: Covici, Friede, 1930.

Jones, Peter, ed. *Imagist Poetry*. Middlesex, England: Penguin Books, 1972.

Pound, Ezra, ed. *Des Imagistes: An Anthology*. New York: Albert and Charles Boni, 1914.

Pratt, William, ed. *The Imagist Poem: Modern Poetry in Miniature*. New York: E. P. Dutton & Co., 1963.

Some Imagist Poets: An Anthology. Boston: Houghton Mifflin Company, 1915.

Some Imagist Poets 1916: An Annual Anthology. Boston: Houghton Mifflin Company, 1916.

Some Imagist Poets 1917: An Annual Anthology. Boston: Houghton Mifflin Company, 1917.

History of the Imagist Movement

Aldington, Richard. "The Imagists." *Bruno Chap Books*. New York: G. Bruno, 1915.

———. *Life for Life's Sake: A Book of Reminiscences*. New York: Viking Press, 1941.

———. "Modern Poetry and the Imagists." *Egoist*, I (June 1, 1914), 201–203.

Coffman, Stanley K., Jr. *Imagism: A Chapter for the History of Modern Poetry*. Norman: University of Oklahoma Press, 1951.

De Chasca, Edmund. *John Gould Fletcher and Imagism*. Columbia: University of Missouri Press, 1978.

Fletcher, Ian. "Some Anticipations of Imagism." *A Catalogue of the Imagist Poets: With Essays by Wallace Martin and Ian Fletcher*. New York: J. Howard Woolmer, 1966.

Fletcher, John Gould. *Life Is My Song*. New York: Farrar & Rinehart, 1937.

Flint, F. S. "The History of Imagism." *Egoist*, II (May 1, 1915), 70–71.

Ford, Ford Madox. "Thus to Revisit." *Dial*, LXIX (August, 1920), 132–41.

————. *Thus to Revisit: Some Reminiscences*. Originally published in 1921. New York: Octagon Books, 1966.

Gould, Jean. *Amy: The World of Amy Lowell and the Imagist Movement*. New York: Dodd, Mead & Company, 1975.

Harmer, J. B. *Victory in Limbo: Imagism 1908–1917*. London: Secker & Warburg, 1975.

Hough, Graham. *Image and Experience: Reflections on a Literary Revolution*. Lincoln: University of Nebraska Press, 1960.

Hughes, Glenn. *Imagism and the Imagists: A Study in Modern Poetry*. Palo Alto: Stanford University Press, 1931.

Jones, A. R. *The Life and Opinions of Thomas Ernest Hulme*. Boston: Beacon Press, 1960.

Kenner, Hugh. *The Pound Era*. Berkeley: University of California Press, 1971.

Lewis, Wyndham. *Blasting and Bombardiering*. Originally published in 1937. Berkeley: University of California Press, 1967.

Lowell, Amy. *Tendencies in Modern American Poetry*. Boston: Houghton Mifflin Company, 1917.

Martin, Wallace. "'The Forgotten School of 1909' and the Origins of Imagism." See Fletcher, Ian.

Perkins, David. *A History of Modern Poetry from the 1890s to the High Modernist Mode*. Cambridge: Harvard University Press, 1976.

Taupin, René. *L'influence du symbolisme francais sur la poesie américaine (de 1910 à 1920)*. Paris: Librairie Ancienne Honoré Champion, 1929.

Other Works Cited

Aldington, Richard. "The Art of Poetry." *Dial*, LXIX (August, 1920), 166–180.

Alleman, Beda. "Metaphor and Anti-Metaphor." *Interpretation: The Poetry of Meaning*. Edited by Stanley Romaine Hopper and David L. Miller. New York: Harcourt, Brace & World, 1967.

Aristotle. *The "Art" of Rhetoric*. Translated by J. H. Freese. Cambridge: Harvard University Press, 1926.

Baker, William E. *Syntax in English Poetry 1870–1930*. Berkeley: University of California Press, 1967.

Barfield, Owen. *Poetic Diction: A Study in Meaning*. Rev. ed. Middletown, Conn.: Wesleyan University Press, 1973.

Bergson, Henri. *An Introduction to Metaphysics*. Translated by T. E. Hulme. New York: G. P. Putnam's Sons, 1912.

———. *Time and Free Will: An Essay on the Immediate Data of Consciousness*. Translated by F. L. Pogson. Originally published in 1910. New York: Harper and Row, 1960.

Booth, Wayne C. *The Rhetoric of Fiction*. Chicago: University of Chicago Press, 1961.

Bradley, A. C. "Poetry for Poetry's Sake." *Oxford Lectures on Poetry*. London: Macmillan and Co., 1909.

Brooke-Rose, Christine. *A Grammar of Metaphor*. London: Secker & Warburg, 1958.

Burke, Kenneth. *Counter-Statement*. Chicago: University of Chicago Press, 1957.

———. *Language as Symbolic Action: Essays on Life, Literature, and Method*. Berkeley: University of California Press, 1966.

———. *A Rhetoric of Motives*. Berkeley: University of California Press, 1969.

Cannell, Skipwith. "The Dance." *New Freewoman*, I (September 1, 1913), 114.

Chisolm, Lawrence. *Fenollosa: The Far East and American Culture*. New Haven: Yale University Press, 1963.

Crane, R. S. *The Languages of Criticism and the Structure of Poetry*. Toronto: University of Toronto Press, 1953.

Culler, Jonathan. *Structuralist Poetics: Structuralism, Linguistics, and the Study of Literature*. Ithaca: Cornell University Press, 1975.

Cunningham, J. V. *Tradition and Poetic Structure: Essays in Literary History and Criticism*. Denver: Alan Swallow Co., 1960.

Davie, Donald. *Articulate Energy: An Inquiry into the Syntax of English Poetry*. London: Routledge & Kegan Paul, 1955.

Dion, Clarice de Sainte Marie. "The Idea of 'Pure Poetry' in English Criticism, 1900–1945." Ph.D. dissertation, The Catholic University of America, 1948.

Eliot, T. S. *American Literature and the American Language*. St. Louis: Washington University Publications, 1953.

———. *Ezra Pound: His Metric and Poetry*. New York: Alfred A. Knopf, 1917.

————. *The Sacred Wood*. Originally published in 1920. London: Methuen & Co., 1960.

————. *Selected Essays*. New ed. New York: Harcourt, Brace & Co., 1960.

Fenollosa, Ernest. *The Chinese Written Character as a Medium for Poetry*. Edited by Ezra Pound. Originally published in 1918. San Francisco: City Lights Books, 1969.

Fish, Stanley. *Self-Consuming Artifacts: The Experience of Seventeenth Century Literature*. Berkeley: University of California Press, 1972.

Fletcher, John Gould. "The Orient in Contemporary Poetry." *The Asian Legacy and American Life*. Edited by Arthur E. Christy. New York: John Day Company, 1945.

Flint, F. S. "Contemporary French Poetry." *Poetry Review*, VII (August, 1912), 355–414.

————. "Imagisme." *Poetry: A Magazine of Verse*, I (January, 1913), 198–200.

Frank, Joseph. "Spatial Form in Literature." *Criticism: The Foundations of Modern Literary Judgment*. Edited by Mark Schorer, Josephine Miles, and Gordon McKenzie. Rev. ed. New York: Harcourt, Brace and Company, 1958.

Frazer, Ray. "The Origin of the Term 'Image.'" *English Literary History*, XXVII (June, 1960), 149–61.

Furbank, P. N. *Reflections on the Word "Image."* London: Secker & Warburg, 1970.

Gourmont, Remy de. "Dust for Sparrows." Translated by Ezra Pound. *Dial*, LXIX (September, October, November, December, 1920), 219–24, 368–71, 484–88, 615–18.

————. *Selected Writings*. Edited and translated by Glenn S. Burne. Ann Arbor: University of Michigan Press, 1966.

Gregory, Joshua C. "Thought and Mental Image, Art and Imitation: A Parallel." *Monist*, XXXI (July, 1921), 420–36.

Hirsch, E. D., Jr. *The Aims of Interpretation*. Chicago: University of Chicago Press, 1976.

————. *Validity in Interpretation*. New Haven: Yale University Press, 1967.

Hornstein, Lillian Herlands. "Analysis of Imagery: A Critique of Method." *PMLA*, LVII (September, 1942), 638–53.

Hulme, T. E. *Further Speculations*. Edited by Sam Hynes. Lincoln: University of Nebraska Press.

————. *Speculations: Essays on Humanism and the Philosophy of Art*. Edited by Herbert Read. London: Routledge & Kegan Paul, 1924.

Juhasz, Suzanne. *Metaphor and the Poetry of Williams, Pound, and Stevens.* Lewisburg, Penn.: Bucknell University Press, 1974.

Kenner, Hugh. *The Art of Poetry.* New York: Rinehart, 1959.

———. *The Poetry of Ezra Pound.* Norfolk, Conn.: New Directions, 1951.

Kermode, Frank. *The Romantic Image.* London: Routledge & Kegan Paul, 1957.

Keynes, John Maynard. "My Early Beliefs." Vol. X of *The Collected Writings of John Maynard Keynes.* London: Macmillan, 1972.

Kitto, H. D. F. *Poiesis: Structure and Thought.* Berkeley: University of California Press, 1966.

Krieger, Murray. *The New Apologists for Poetry.* Minneapolis: University of Minnesota Press, 1956.

Langbaum, Robert. *The Poetry of Experience: The Dramatic Monologue in Modern Literary Tradition.* New York: W. W. Norton & Company, 1957.

Lowell, Amy. "A Consideration of Modern Poetry." *North American Review,* CCV (January, 1917), 103–17.

———. "Mr. Fletcher's Verse." *New Republic,* III (May 15, 1915), 48–49.

———. "The New Manner in Modern Poetry." *New Republic,* VIII (March 4, 1916), 124–25.

Lowes, John Livingston. *Convention and Revolt in Poetry.* London: Constable & Co., 1919.

Martin, Wallace. "The Sources of the Imagist Aesthetic." *PMLA,* LXXXV (March, 1970), 196–204.

Miles, Josephine. *Eras and Modes in English Poetry.* Berkeley: University of California Press, 1964.

———. "The Problem of Imagery." *Sewanee Review,* LVIII (Summer, 1950), 522–26.

———. "Reading Poems." *English Journal,* LII (March, April, 1963), 157–64, 243–46.

Miner, Earl. "Pound, *Haiku,* and the Image." *Hudson Review,* IX (Winter, 1956–1957), 570–84.

Monroe, Harriet. "Introduction." *The New Poetry: An Anthology.* Edited by Harriet Monroe and Alice Corbin Henderson. New York: Macmillan Company, 1920.

Moore, Arthur K. *Contestable Concepts of Literary Theory.* Baton Rouge: Louisiana State University Press, 1973.

Nagy, N. Christophe de. *Ezra Pound's Poetics and Literary Tradition.* Bern: Francke, 1966.

Nänny, Max. *Ezra Pound: Poetics for an Electric Age.* Bern: Francke, 1973.

Nemerov, Howard. *Figures of Thought: Speculations on the Meaning of Poetry and Other Essays*. Boston: David R. Godine, 1978.

Olson, Elder. "The Poetic Process." *Critical Inquiry*, II (Autumn, 1975), 69–74.

Pater, Walter. *Selected Writings of Walter Pater*. Edited by Harold Bloom. New York: American Library, 1974.

Perelman, Chaim, and L. Olbrechts-Tyteca. *The New Rhetoric: A Treatise on Argumentation*. Translated by John Wilkinson and Purcell Weaver. Notre Dame: University of Notre Dame Press, 1969.

Perrine, Laurence. *Sound and Sense: An Introduction to Poetry*. 4th ed. New York: Harcourt Brace Jovanovich, 1973.

Pound, Ezra. *ABC of Reading*. Originally published 1934. New York: New Directions, 1960.

———. *Gaudier-Brzeska: A Memoir*. Originally published 1916. New York: New Directions, 1970.

———. "How I Began." *Ezra Pound: Perspectives*. Edited by Noel Stock. Chicago: Henry Regnery Co., 1965.

———. *Literary Essays of Ezra Pound*. Edited by T. S. Eliot. New York: New Directions, 1968.

———. "On Criticism in General." *Criterion*, I (January, 1923), 143–56.

———. *The Selected Letters of Ezra Pound: 1907–1941*. Edited by D. D. Paige. New York: New Directions, 1971.

———. *The Spirit of Romance*. Originally published 1910. New York: New Directions, n.d.

———. "Status Rerum." *Poetry: A Magazine of Verse*, I (January, 1913), 123–27.

———. "The Wisdom of Poetry." *Forum*, XLVII (April, 1912), 497–501.

Ramsey, Warren. "Pound, LaForgue, and Dramatic Structure." *Comparative Literature*, III (Winter, 1951), 47–56.

Read, Herbert. *The Tenth Muse*. London: Routledge & Kegan Paul, 1957.

Richards, I. A. *Coleridge on Imagination*. Originally published in 1934. Bloomington: Indiana University Press, 1960.

———. *Practical Criticism: A Study of Literary Judgment*. Originally published in 1928. New York: Harcourt, Brace & World, 1964.

Riding, Laura. *Contemporaries and Snobs*. New York: Doubleday Doran & Co., 1928.

Schneidau, Herbert N. *Ezra Pound: The Image and the Real*. Baton Rouge: Louisiana State University Press, 1969.

Shelley, Percy Bysshe. *A Defence of Poetry*. Edited by John E. Jordon. New York: Bobbs-Merrill Company, 1965.

Smith, Barbara Herrnstein. *Poetic Closure: A Study of How Poems End*. Chicago: University of Chicago Press, 1968.

Stevens, Wallace. *The Necessary Angel: Essays on Reality and the Imagination*. New York: Alfred A. Knopf, 1951.

Sutton, Walter. "The Literary Image and the Reader: A Consideration of the Theory of Spatial Form." *Journal of Aesthetics and Art Criticism*, XVI (September, 1957), 112–23.

Symons, Arthur. *The Symbolist Movement in Literature*. Originally published in 1899. New York: E. P. Dutton and Co., 1958.

Winters, Yvor. *In Defense of Reason*. 3rd ed. Chicago: The Swallow Press, 1947.

———. *The Uncollected Essays and Reviews of Yvor Winters*. Edited by Francis Murphy. Chicago: Swallow Press, 1973.

Witemeyer, Hugh. *The Poetry of Ezra Pound: Forms and Renewal, 1908–1920*. Berkeley: University of California Press, 1969.

Wordsworth, William. *Wordsworth: Poetical Works*. Edited by Thomas Hutchinson. New ed. revised by Ernest de Selincourt. Oxford: Clarendon Press, 1969.

Wright, George T. *The Poet in the Poem: The Personae of Eliot, Yeats, and Pound*. Berkeley: University of California Press, 1962.

Yeats, John Butler. *Passages from the Letters of John Butler Yeats: Selected by Ezra Pound*. Churchtown, Dundrum: Cuala Press, 1917.

Yeats, William Butler. *Essays and Introductions*. New York: Macmillan Company, 1961.

———. "Introduction." *The Oxford Book of Modern Verse*. Edited by John Hollander. Oxford: Oxford University Press, 1968.

INDEX